OTHER TITLES PUBLISHED BY
TEXAS FISH & GAME PUBLISHING CO., LLC

Books:
Saltwater Strategies®: Texas Trout Tactics
by Chester Moore, Jr.

Texas Fish & Game's Saltwater Strategies®:
Pat Murray's No-Nonsense Guide to
Coastal Fishing

Texas Saltwater Classics:
Fly Patterns for the Texas Coast
by Greg Berlocher

Saltwater Strategies®: Flounder Fundamentals
by Chester Moore, Jr.

Doreen's 24 Hour Eat Gas Now Café
by Reavis Z. Wortham

Periodicals:
Texas Fish & Game magazine (12x/year)

Texas Lakes & Bays Atlas (annual)

Texas Hunting (annual)

for information, contact us at:
1-800-750-4678
www.fishgame.com

Texas Fish & Game Publishing Co., LLC
2350 North Sam Houston Parkway East, Suite 240
Houston, Texas 77032
1-800-750-4678 • Fax: 713-227-3002

Texas Fish & Game's

SALTWATER STRATEGIES®
BOOK SERIES PRESENTS

TEXAS REDS

By Chester Moore, Jr.

**Texas Fish & Game
Publishing Co., L.L.C.**

2350 North Sam Houston Parkway E., Suite 240
Houston, Texas 77032
1-800-750-4678
Website: www.fishgame.com

Published by

**Texas Fish & Game
Publishing Co., L.L.C.**
2350 North Sam Houston Parkway East, Suite 240
Houston Texas 77032
Phone: 281-227-3001 Fax: 281-227-3002
Website: www.fishgame.com

First Edition

Cover photo by George Knighten

Foreword by Ed Holder

Edited by Don Zaidle

All photos by Chester Moore, Jr., unless otherwise credited.

Production design by Wendy Kipfmiller

Layout by Doug Berry

ISBN: 0-929980-15-8

DEDICATION

This book is dedicated to the brave men and women of the US armed forces who give their all to ensure our fishing freedom.

Contents

Foreword

A Fishy Writer

Readers of this and other books written by Chester Moore might wonder if he is a writer/fisherman or fisherman/writer. That's a difficult question to answer because he's a writer who loves to fish and a fisherman who loves to write. One thing is clear, however: the two loves have produced a writer who knows his subject.

Chester grew up a bicycle ride from coastal estuaries where redfish roamed. He was introduced to these bullies of brackish water at an early age and has been chasing them ever since. That chase has carried him from his bicycle waters to many coastal bays and out into the Gulf of Mexico and taught him much about redfish. He shares his knowledge in this book.

He does it with an easy-going style anglers can understand and appreciate, whether they are inexperienced beginners or "old salts"; whether they have expensive boating rigs or do their fishing from the bank; whether they like to feed redfish various baits or fool them with lures. He even offers some proven recipes for cooking redfish, and digs into conservation issues important to those who like to catch redfish.

He also does it with the enthusiasm of a dedicated fisherman—and writer. There I go again. But you decide after reading the book. Is he a writer/fisherman or fisherman/writer? —*Ed Holder*

Introduction

The water on Keith Lake was dead calm, except for a tiny ripple 20 yards away.

"Throw there," said my fishing partner, outdoor writer Ed Holder. "There's a school of redfish just below the surface."

I saw the ripple, but could not make out the reds. Having great faith in my partner's knowledge of the area, I chucked a bone-colored Rebel Jumpin' Minnow toward the wrinkle.

Wham!

A massive school of reds boiled below the plug, several specimens attacking it at once. They hit it so hard that it sailed five feet from the water, and then they struck it again upon landing. These reds were trying hard, and this time one of them got a mouthful of treble hooks for its efforts. Seconds later, Holder connected and we had a double mere minutes into our trip. By the time we landed those reds, the school moved on, and so did we.

Our next stop was a shallow flat hidden deep in the expansive, brackish marsh. The water was clear and we could see the reds swimming around along with sheepshead and mullet. It was a heavenly sight that made me thankful for being born on the Gulf Coast.

As I took it all in, Holder gave me protocol: "Your best bet here is to throw just in front of the reds and let them come up to it. Walk the bait real good and they'll go crazy."

I did just as he instructed and immediately hooked a nice, triple-spotted redfish. In the ultra-shallow water, its battle was impressive. The big, beautiful fish made determined runs and disturbed the water with its broad, blue-tinged tail. It was truly beautiful.

That day will live in my memory forever.

It was then that my lifelong love for redfish took on new meaning and Mother Nature planted the seeds for me to write this book.

I have always regarded redfish in high esteem, but that trip gave me newfound respect for the species. Redfish are beautiful, fight hard, and have some of the tastiest flesh in the sea. Some of my earliest childhood memories are of rolling redfish in cracker meal for family fish fries. I can almost taste the golden brown fillets delighting my taste buds, along with homemade French fries and coleslaw. Redfish fries were a family tradition and one that carries on to this day, the only difference being Dad now delegates me to cleaning duties while he gets the comfortable battering gig.

Tradition is something that surrounds redfish more than any inland game species. I admit that flounder are my favorite, and speckled trout get more attention from the outdoor media, but redfish have a certain aura about them. A vibe goes along with pursuing them. It was evident on the water that day with Holder and is ingrained in my father, who spent hundreds of days pursuing reds in the coastal marshes around Sabine Lake, Lake Calcasieu, and

PHOTO BY GEORGE KNIGHTEN

Spotting a "tailing" redfish is one of the most thrilling experiences on the Gulf Coast

Rollover Pass.

Long before the speckled trout was the most popular species on the Gulf Coast, redfish were the big prize. As recently as the mid 1980's, anglers greeted reports of big trout catches with far less enthusiasm than tales of tailing reds in the shallow flats. In my region, trout were mainly by-catch for anglers seeking reds.

How times have changed. Now, some diehard speckled trout anglers give redfish disparaging nicknames like "golden croaker on steroids," "crab carp," and "fool's gold." I personally want to puke when I hear anglers disrespecting redfish; to me, those comments are trampling on the traditions of many great anglers.

Most redfish experts do not participate in the Gulf Coast Troutmasters or wear designer fishing clothes. In fact, you are likely to see them donning white shrimping boots and a welder's cap.

On the other hand, some of the most affluent anglers on the

Gulf Coast have found a deep appreciation for the redfish in recent years. Texas fly-fishermen have taken to the species, giving them the same status as bonefish in the Caribbean: kings of the flats.

This makes today an interesting time for redfish. They are no longer the most popular fish on the Texas coast, but they have a loyal fan base that includes some of the most skilled and under-appreciated anglers in the world.

I dedicate this book to keeping their traditions alive and showing those new to coastal fishing that redfish are tremendous fun to pursue, catch, and eat.

Thank God for the redfish!

Chapter One

Life of the Redfish

The red drum, *Sciaenops ocellatus*, is a fish of many monikers. Most anglers in Texas and Louisiana call it "redfish", but some call it "channel bass" in parts of Florida, and *"pescado colorado"* or simply *"colorado"* in Mexico.

Redfish, as I will identify them throughout this book, also get names for different age classes. "Rat red" signifies juveniles whereas the term "bull red" applies to big, sexually mature specimens.

As a kid, I used to get a real kick out of the tag "channel bass" because I had a Lone Star Beer "Saltwater Fish of Texas" poster that had that name listed under the redfish. To this day, I cannot figure where the "bass" part came in. They look nothing like a largemouth (assuming the namer had that species in mind), and their fight puts to shame anything from freshwater of comparable size.

The best description I have found for the physical traits and habits of the species is from a study entitled: "The Red Drum in

Texas" by James A. Dailey, Coastal Fisheries Division, Texas Parks & Wildlife Department (TPWD).

> The red drum is a member of the drum family whose cousins include the Atlantic croaker, spot, spotted seatrout, and black drum. The most distinguishing mark on the red drum is one large black spot on the upper part of the tail base. Having multiple spots is not uncommon for this fish but having no spots is extremely rare. The color of red drum ranges from a deep blackish, coppery color to nearly silver. The most common color is reddish-bronze.

I disagree with that last sentence. A redfish is bronze, but I cannot find any red to them at all. We should call them "bronzefish." That would make a lot more sense, but what do I know?

The species is fast growing, reaching approximately 11 inches and 1 pound in its first year, 17-22 inches and 3-1/2 pounds in two years, and 22-24 inches and 6-8 pounds in three years. The world record red drum weighed 96 pounds and hailed from the East coast. The current Texas record is 55 pounds.

> Red drum reach sexual maturity between their third and fourth years when they are about thirty inches long. They spawn in the Gulf, possibly near the mouths of passes. On the Texas coast spawning occurs generally from mid-August through mid-October. Eggs hatch within 24 hours and are carried into the bays by tidal current. The larval red drum

Redfish feed on everything from blue crabs to mullet pictured here. Mullet is one of the standby baits for reds.

seeks quiet, shallow water with grassy or muddy bottoms.

For the first three years, redfish live in the bays or in the surf zone near passes and jetties. Evidence from TPWD's tag returns show that they remain in the same area and generally move less than three miles from where fisheries officials tag them. I know this firsthand.

In June 2001, while fishing the Texas side of the Sabine jetties with Bill Killian of Orange, Texas, I caught a redfish that I had tagged more than three weeks earlier at the cluster of rigs located just east of the jetties. I was hoping other anglers would catch some of the fish I had tagged, but never thought *I* would.

Nasty green algae covered the tag, but it was easy to read after I wiped it off. The tag's number was 31. The big red was caught and released like all others that day and perhaps to be caught again by another angler. The chances of catching one's own tagged fish has to be miniscule, but it proved these fish do not move much.

As they mature, they move from the bays to the Gulf of Mexico where they remain the rest of

The barnacle-encrusted structure of oil platforms is a magnet for big bull redfish.

their lives, except for infrequent visits to the bays. Although there is little evidence of seasonal migrations, anglers find concentrations of red drum in rivers and tidal creeks during the winter. Daily movement from the shallows to deeper waters is influenced by tides and water temperatures.

During the fall, especially during stormy weather, large adult red drum move to the Gulf beaches, possibly for spawning, where they can be caught from piers and by surf anglers. Anglers call this the "bull redfish run."

Juvenile redfish feed mainly on small crab, shrimp, and marine worms. As they mature, they move on to larger crab, shrimp, and small fish. They are designed to feed on the bottom, but will feed anywhere in the water column when the opportunity arises. In a later chapter, you will read about the incredible phenomenon of schooling redfish where hundreds of them gather and destroy anything in their path. Sometimes this happens in 50 feet of water in the Gulf of Mexico, and at other times in super shallow areas.

Another phenomenon is "tailing," which involves the reds' tails sticking out of the water as they feed in the shallows. In some areas, anglers should call this "backing" because you see a lot more back and dorsal fin than spotted tail at a 45-degree angle. Either way, it is badass in my book.

Redfish prefer salty areas, but do just fine in pure freshwater marsh. In fact, my mentor, Ed Holder, sight-casts to them in an area where they swim with channel catfish and largemouth bass.

TPWD has successfully stocked them in several freshwater reservoirs including Fairfield, Braunig, and Calaveras. They cannot spawn in these lakes, but they grow to immense size and take to the habitat like, well, a fish takes to water. Instead of feeding on crab, they eat crawfish and terrorize the perch, shad, bass, and other wimpy freshwater species.

Redfish are highly adaptable, and this allows them to survive in many habitats and live to great age. According to the North Carolina Department of Environment and Fisheries, the oldest recorded specimen was 62 years old, caught in the Atlantic Ocean.

Ocean-going redfish are still a mystery to scientists. As detailed previously, the juveniles are supposed to spend their first three years inshore, but anglers routinely catch juveniles offshore. I have caught reds in the 20 to 28-inch class as far as 40 miles offshore. This obviously represents a segment of the population scientists have not figured out yet, and that puts them in the same boat with anglers.

This book has many tips for catching these highly sporting fish, but as any dedicated pursuer of redfish knows, they always have a surprise up their gills.

Chapter Two

Seasonal Patterns & Tactics:

The beautiful thing about redfish is anglers can catch them with relative ease throughout the year. The biggest segment of the flounder population leaves the bays during winter, and speckled trout simply get lockjaw, but it seems like redfish are always biting somewhere.

I remember freezing my butt off while fishing off the side of the road with my dad during the winter catching one redfish after another. People thought we were crazy, but winter is a great time to catch reds—and so are spring, summer, and fall.

Let's look at the best tactics and locations for redfish throughout the seasons.

SPRING

Redfish dwell in shallow areas year-round. During certain times of year, they take to the main water or inhabit deep areas in

Dave Concienne holds a nice speck and redfish. During spring, anglers should target shallow shorelines.

ship channels, but there are always reds in the shallows.

Target springtime reds around shorelines adjacent to cuts in the marshes and along mud flats. In the early part of March, the water is still rather cool and shallow mud flats near deep water, like ship channels, hold many reds on warm, sunny afternoons. The black mud holds heat, which brings in baitfishes, which in turn

"Wild" Bill Skinner hoists two massive redfish he caught while fishing with the author at the Sabine Jetties. Actually, the author caught one and he caught the other at the same time.

bring in reds.

Oyster reefs are one of the most overlooked areas to target redfish during spring. That may be because understanding and fishing oyster reefs is complex. Anglers have to consider everything from depth, tidal movement, and predator-prey relations to water clarity and the all-important influx of freshwater.

Texas bay systems, particularly those on the Upper Coast, are prone to flooding in the spring. The flooding, in fact, can get so bad that surface water miles out into the Gulf of Mexico can be almost purely fresh.

Redfish are very tolerant of freshwater, but they typically concentrate in heavier numbers in saltwater during flooded periods. Saltwater is heavier than freshwater so it goes to the bottom and that is where the redfish will be. The deepest water will be the saltiest water, and in ecosystems like Galveston Bay and Sabine Lake, many of the oyster reefs are in deep water. Reefs on the southern end of bays are especially good places to look for redfish because they have a strong tidal flow, which brings in saltier water from the Gulf. During spring floods, oyster reefs covered by deep water are loaded with redfish.

Oyster reefs are unique ecosystems. In open, barren bay sys-

Anglers should photograph exposed structures like this oyster reef during periods of low tide so they can better fish them when the tide is high.

tems typical of Texas, they are like an oasis in the desert. They are great spots for small baitfishes to seek refuge and prey on microorganisms. This is turn makes them great places to contact opportunistic predators like redfish.

Oyster reefs harbor your typical batfishes like mullet, menhaden, glass minnows, and crab, but they also attract some unusual species. Sand eels are one of the most prolific baitfish species that inhabit oyster reefs, and they are a favorite prey item of redfish. This is especially true during April, when the menhaden are small and shrimp are hard to find. It is a rare occurrence to catch a redfish during this time that does not have sand eels in its belly. This should be a clue to anglers.

James France, formerly of Catch-Em Lures, said a good way to catch these eel-loving redfish is with a Sabine Snake: "The company I used to own still produces the Sabine Snake, which is a bait that was designed years ago to catch redfish on reefs. Sometimes, when they are feeding on the eels, they do not want anything else. That is when the Snake becomes a real go-to bait."

I have fished on reefs numerous times and had great success with the fire tiger and junebug colors. The lure has incredible action and successfully mimics the herky-jerky movements of a sand eel.

The Norton Sand Eel is another good sand eel imitator. This bait has come on strong in the last couple of years, and comes in a variety of colors for various water conditions and personal preferences.

During drought years, cutlass fish, also known as ribbonfish, are common on oyster reefs and redfish will absolutely gorge themselves on them. Good cutlass fish imitations include the Redfish Assassin, Slug-go, and Mr. Twister Slimy Slug. The latter is a favorite choice of Matagorda Bay guide Capt. Don Wood. Matagorda, by the

PHOTO BY: GEORGE KNIGHTEN

Sand-eel imitators like the Bass Assassin are killer for red-fish.

way, has some first-class oyster reefs harboring huge redfish.

The most important thing to keep in mind about any of these lures is to fish them on a heavy jighead. Fishing with 1/8- and 1/4-ounce jigheads may give a lure a more life-like appearance, but you need something that will get down to the bottom and help fight heavy spring currents. I would go with at least a 3/8-ounce jighead, but actually prefer a 1/2-ounce head. Remember, you cannot catch fish unless they can see or hear the lure.

Drift with the current and let the lure bounce, bump, and crash into the oyster reef. Water conditions during spring usually range from off-colored to murky to just plain nasty, so anything that might grab the attention of a redfish is worth trying.

Make sure you have enough line out so that you are not fishing vertically. The lure will not work properly that way. In addition, it is important to keep contact with the lure. Springtime redfish are not overly aggressive and often hit soft plastic lures lightly. Use a super sensitive monofilament or braided line for best results.

It is important to remember that Mother Nature did not create equal oyster reefs, and she did not make reefs just one big, flat block of oysters. You want to look for structure within the structure. An oyster reef is a structure all by itself, but there is structure on top of that structure. A big clump of oysters rising up on a slight ridge on a reef with an average depth of 10 feet is structure on structure. A sunken boat on a reef is structure on structure.

It is very important to keep watch for drop-offs. A ledge that drops off to 16 feet on a 10 feet deep reef is a hot fishing spot. These are the places redfish gang up to intercept baitfishes. If you just jump over these spots without letting out extra line, you may not reach the fish. Keep your electronics on and look for the drop-off. When you hit it, let out some extra line and you will probably catch fish.

An indispensable tool in reef fishing is a marker buoy. You can purchase them at a tackle store or simply make your own with 2-liter cola bottles. When coming across a hotspot, throw out the buoys so you can return there. There might be 200 fish bunched up in a 20-yard spot, and that may be where they stay all day. You must be able to stay within the bite window to be successful.

SUMMER

Calm, slick days mean schooling redfish during summer. I have dedicated an entire chapter to fishing for schooling redfish else-where in this book, but it is worth brief mention here. Schooling reds are one of the most magnificent sights this outdoor writer has ever seen—and I have fished everywhere from Venezuela to Venice, Louisiana. These reds gather by the acre in the nearshore Gulf of

Is there a redfish in this picture? Oh yes, but with the beautiful woman it is somewhat hard to tell, isn't it? This nice Lake Calcasieu red fell to a topwater thrown along a protected shoreline.

Mexico and in the bays. The largest school I have seen covered an area of about three acres; redfish were everywhere.

It does not take rocket science to find these fish. When they are feeding on top, they look like a nuclear submarine rising from the abyss. Moreover, when they are just cruising around, the water around them takes on a glorious bronze tint.

"One thing that happens when people get into the big bull reds is they usually end up wearing themselves out," said Capt. Tim Bradbeer, a Texas bull redfish specialist. "They got so excited catching the first few fish, and then after a half dozen or so, their muscles are aching, but they love every minute of it. I guarantee that."

Targeting redfish in the marsh is another viable option during summer. Look for reds along grassy shorelines and in areas where a hard bottom meets soft bottom. The best way to locate such areas without getting in the water and feeling around is to look for roseau cane. It grows on harder bottoms, so the area around it is a prime place to hunt reds. Roseau cane's rooting system holds lots of crabs and that is a redfish favorite.

In super shallow water, look for "tailing" redfish, which are simply reds with their tails sticking out of the water. As detailed in the topwater chapter, cast directly in front of redfish for the best chance of getting a strike. Topwaters and spoons are the best lures for this practice.

Besides catching them schooling, my favorite way to find summer reds is at night. Look for shallow flats adjacent to deep water. These flats hold lots of baitfishes at night, which attracts reds. Crab is the best bait for redfish in these areas. Broken in half and hooked through the carapace, crab has a long hook life and is irresistible to reds. Squid is sometimes used, as is jumbo shrimp, but my favorite is live croaker. Live croaker is better for offshore, but it works in bays as well. The usual drill involves throwing a couple of rods out in the flats and then one in the nearby deep water. The shallows produce most of the fish, but occasionally the deep gives up a trophy-sized fish.

FALL

Bull redfish excite me and I do not care who knows it. As I have written in *Texas Fish & Game* magazine and other publications, the big, beautiful bronze beasts stir my soul with each glorious encounter. There is something about them that hits me at a spiritual level.

A Chug Bug fooled this massive bull redfish caught by wildlife photographer Gerald Burleigh.

This dates back to the first time I ever saw one at Meacom's Pier on the Bolivar Peninsula. As the full moon shined over the calm, clear surf, I noticed a hint of bronze in the water. It was massive bull red swimming under the lights of the pier. For years, I had heard the tales of hard-fighting, gigantic redfish, but this was my first-ever personal encounter. To a youngster who obsessed over such things, it was like coming face to face with a legend. I was in love.

After that first red appeared, it did not take long for others to join it and cause line alarms to sing send fishermen rushing to their rods. I stood amidst the excitement and prayed I would feel the same many more times. I craved an encounter with a bull redfish then, and I crave one now.

Fortunately, there are plenty of opportunities to encounter these prized sport fish on the Texas coast during the fall months. They have made a strong comeback since the government stopped commercial harvest more than 20 years ago, and pier fishing is not just viable but highly productive. Most pier anglers use lengthy surf rods that allow for long distance casting. These are especially helpful to anglers who do not like crowded piers and prefer the solace of lonely surf. A surf rod helps them get their bait past the first couple of sandbars. Do not be afraid to go after reds on piers if you do not have a surf rod. I have seen several anglers land reds on tackle ranging from Penn Senators rigged on short offshore sticks to an Ambassador 6500 attached to a popping rod. If you are proficient at playing big fish, you should be able to land a red on most any gear. Just set your drag accordingly.

Should you choose to fish areas of the surf where there are no piers, look for structure. Structure is the key to locating the greatest concentration of fish. Just setting up on a stretch of beach because it looks pretty will not necessarily be productive for bull redfish. The first thing to look for is points. The classic point configuration extends out at right angles to the beach. Sometimes the beach curves and it may look more like a "bend," but this is still a point.

Sometimes, small submerged points are practically invisible to the naked eye, but anglers can spot them by looking for small "rips" close to the beach. It is usually best to fish the water sweeping past points or right at the tip. Other good point-related locations include the sloping sides, which anglers sometimes call "pockets" because they appear as scooped out impressions from the base of a point on both sides. Pockets often hold many crustaceans, which in turn draw in redfish.

Bowls are another kind of structure to look for when searching for fish in the surf. Bowls indent into the shore and form between two points. They are usually subtler than a point, but can still hold tremendous numbers of redfish. I have little experience fishing for redfish in the surf, but have had success on a couple of

Diana Suire caught this huge bull redfish in the surf during the heat of summer.

occasions at a deep bowl located near High Island.

Troughs are the most commonly mentioned structure in the surf-fishing game. They are simply impressions that run parallel to sand bars and provide means for fish to travel down the surf. Fish tend to feed along the sides of a trough rather than in its center, especially in spots where the trough drops off steeply from shallow water. Find these spots and you will usually find fish.

Piers and surf are fine places to catch bull reds, but there is no better place than at the jetty systems that lead into Texas bays and the nearshore Gulf. Jetties draw redfish in like a moth to flame and are easy to pattern, especially during fall. For anglers new to jetty fishing, I will keep it simple.

To catch bull reds at the jetties, find the deep holes on the Gulf or ship channel side. These holes will hold as many redfish as you can handle. I have caught as many as 15 of the brutes in one hole at the Sabine jetties, and had similar success at Galveston and Surfside. The best spot to look is at the southern tip of the jetty where it opens up to the Gulf. The current causes deep washouts where the wall divides the Gulf and ship channel. These spots are usually loaded with reds. Another good spot is the boat cut, which provide a strong tidal exchange and a buffet of crab and baitfishes.

In the nearshore Gulf out to a couple of miles, it is possible to encounter schooling bull redfish. I have seen schools as large as an Academy store parking lot. You will notice these schools because they make about as much commotion as a surfacing nuclear submarine. It is a beautiful sight. These schooling reds will hit just about anything you throw at them, but I would advise live croaker or mullet along with 1/2-ounce silver spoons and Rat-L-Traps. As I noted previously, these schooling reds can be spooky. I find them even more so in the fall. They may seem fearless as they madly thrash the surface, but they are actually a very spooky fish. If you see schooling reds, cut your motor a long way from them and switch over to your trolling motor. If the reds go under, approach the area where you last saw them and begin drifting. Sometimes they will follow the current to catch up with whatever they are feeding on, so drifting is a good way to find them without spooking. Starting up the big motor could mess things up.

Another option is the short rigs off Crystal Beach. These rigs are stacked with oversized redfish during fall, and many of them are located within state waters where the government allows you to possess redfish. Keeping reds is illegal in federal waters of the Gulf of Mexico.

Lisa Moore caught her first ever bull redfish while fishing in the middle of a thunderstorm at Meacom's Pier.

My favorite bull redfish bait is live croaker, hand down, without a doubt. Cut mullet fished on the bottom is also a good way to bag these redfish, but sometimes they seem to prefer suspended bait. In this case, fish with a mullet or whole blue crab on a free-line. I frequently catch bull reds this way on the same setup I use for sharks in the summer. I use a 4-foot steel leader finished off with a Daiichi Tru-Turn hook. The leader offers some protection from the pilings of the rigs and the circle hook allows me to catch and release big reds without harming them; most of the time, the circle hook lodges in the corner of the red's mouth. If you have never used circle hooks, I would recommend placing the rod in a holder and allowing the fish to hook itself. Do not try to set the hook as you would with a regular J-style hook. After the rod starts bending, over give it a slight tug and start reeling in. You will actually catch more fish this way than you will would with a j style-hook.

Using chum can greatly aid catching big redfish. Most anglers do not utilize chum when seeking reds, but I have found it very useful. I always hang a lingerie bag filled with mashed menhaden over the side to attract fish.

To catch these massive reds on lures, a 1-ounce gold spoon chunked toward the platform legs can be a real killer. Throw out about 10 feet from the leg and let it slowly flutter down.

No matter where you catch them, something to keep in mind with bull reds is they are highly stressed after a vigorous battle. If you plan to release it, get it back in the water as soon as possible. When fishing from a pier, use a drop net to bob the fish up and down to help get some oxygen going through its gills. In addition, check to see if the fish has a distended air bladder. If so, pop it with a fillet knife or other sharp object. This will help increase the chances of survival.

To take slot-size redfish, target the main body of the bay and look for them feeding under birds. It will be difficult to tell whether reds or trout are feeding, but either way you cannot lose.

When the big blue northers come through, look to the cuts emptying the marsh to produce the most redfish. When the water leaves the marsh, so does everything that lives there, and this creates a buffet for big reds. Look for slight drop-offs just outside of cuts to hold the most redfish.

WINTER

Finding big concentrations of redfish in winter can be tough. Fish are cold-blooded and do not really like winter. They seek sanctuary from winter weather, which is why warm water outfall canals are such great fishing holes. Along the Texas coast, there are several warm water discharges from energy plants and refineries that can harbor incredible numbers of fish.

I grew up fishing around the Entergy Plant near Bridge City. It is like several similar outfits along the Texas Gulf Coast in that it cools its turbines by pumping water from one canal and expelling it into another. In this case, the water is coming from a marsh bordering the Lower Neches Wildlife Management Area and is exiting into a canal that leads to the mouth of the Neches River. Both usually hold salty water during winter. Baitfishes congregate in such warm waters during cold spells, making a buffet for a host of large predators. They are great for human predators, too, since the cold-blooded fish become more active feeders in these warm spots.

Warm-water discharges come in many forms. They can be a huge cooling plant that spews out thousands of gallons of warm water a minute, or they can be a small drainage pipe or culvert that has a very light flow. Chemical refineries often have small pump stations that produce warm water flow that diverts into underwater pipes.

Any of these areas can hold a surprising amount of fish. The more flow and the warmer the water compared to the surrounding waters, the more fish there will be. An interesting phenomenon in

During winter redfish tend to stick around warmwater discharges and in deep areas. This angler caught this particular specimen on Sabine Lake.

these areas is that different species favor various degrees of warmth or current. For example, redfish congregate next to the outflow pipes and prefer areas where the water is warmest. The deeper holes in the canal may also hold many reds. Dead shrimp will catch a mess of small reds, but use cut mullet or crab if you are after big ones. I have found squid an effective alternative. It has the right smell and its almost luminescent color adds visual appeal in dark water.

Something to keep in mind is that even small flows from a single drainpipe can draw fish. They may not hold massive schools of fish for long periods, but even a slight change in water temperature can make a big difference in cold weather. It is very important to look for the little things in these spots, since very often that is all it takes to attract game fish. One of the outfall canals I fish does not even pump hot water anymore, but the fish still congregate there. Old timers in the area say the fish in the area are "programmed" to go there. If that is true, then Mother Nature must program bull redfish to hit the jetties during winter. I grew up believing they only came nearshore during the fall, but found out there are plenty for anglers to find during winter at the jetties.

The largest concentrations of redfish seem to be at the deep holes at the southern tip of the Gulf side of jetties. If for some reason the deeper holes are inaccessible, you should back off and look for dips in the rocks. These dips indicate deep holes, and that is where the redfish will be. Another sign is vegetation growing on the bottom of the rocks. These areas hold lots of small crab, which makes excellent redfish bait. Shrimp is good, too. The advantage of using shrimp is that it is readily available, whereas crab can be tough to come by. Shrimp has one serious drawback though. Everything in the ocean eats it, so sometimes a redfish does not get a chance to get the bait.

I generally put out several lines with a slip egg weight and swivel, finished off with a wide gapped hook. This simple set up is ideal for catching reds, but knowing when to set the hook is another issue entirely. For some reason, bull redfish like to peck on bait during winter. Other times of year, they slam whatever you throw at them with great fury, but during winter, they peck for a while and then take off. The best setup is to place the rod in a holder and turn on the reel clicker. When the clicker starts to sound, turn it off and reel in the slack. When it feels like your rod is water bound, set the hook.

A few years ago, a letter from a reader led me to a spot at the Sabine Jetties where slot-size redfish were gathered around large concentrations of menhaden and suspended in 25 feet of water. By running my fish-finder, it did not take long to find the shad. There were millions of them as the entire middle section of the screen looked like a solid piece of structure. I put on a live menhaden, slowly lowered it to the desired depth, and immediately got a strike. My rod bent in half and I was battling a nice redfish. After landing that fish, I quickly hooked up with another and ended up catching 20 between 23 and 36 inches. Some might say I was a lunatic for being on the water that day—the air temperature was in the mid 30s and the wind chill had to be in the upper teens.

Truly understanding jetties is crucial to being able to catch fish there. They might look like a simple pile of useless rocks, but there is more to it than that. To start with, the rocks are three times wider at the bottom than they are at the surface, which means you have more structure than meets the eye. The real structure is below the surface—pockets in the rocks and deep holes that create eddies and strong currents.

It is crucial to move until you find fish. During winter months, I never give one spot more than 20 minutes if I have not caught a sheepshead, redfish, redfish, or redfish. Fish are gregarious, especially during winter and the angler who finds one fish should find much more where that one came from.

When fishing jetties from a boat, anchoring technique is a

major issue. Use lots of rope. About 125 feet should be enough. Between the rope and anchor there should be at least five feet of heavy chain. This helps keep the anchor on the bottom. Never shut off the engine while anchoring. You could easily drift into the rocks and cause severe damage to your boat and possibly yourself. Keep the boat upcurrent from the intended fishing hole and then drop the anchor. I have been using an anchor called the Mighty-Mite and have found it the ultimate jetty anchor. It has specially designed teeth that provide a steady grip but still dislodge from just about any rocky crevice with relative ease.

Chapter Three

Reds on Top are Tops

Redfish are to topwater plugs what A-10 Warthogs are to Iraqi tanks: destruction. Reds do not just "hit" a plug, they strike it with such great force you would think they have some personal beef with it. Trout "smack" or "slurp" topwaters, whereas reds pounce like a cougar on an unwary whitetail. I have always said that if anglers consider what trout do a "blowup," they should call a topwater redfish strike "nuclear holocaust."

Despite the dramatics, most anglers' experiences with reds on topwaters come while pursuing speckled trout. The scenario usually goes something like this: An eager angler walks a Top Dog along a promising piece of shoreline. It is where his friend caught a 10-pounder last week and he hopes its siblings are still in the area. As his mind focuses on walking the dog just right, a mighty explosion rocks the surface. The rod doubles over and the fisherman's heart races as his dreams of catching a double-digit trout seem within

TEXAS FISH & GAME

Chugging-style topwater plugs are tops for big redfish.

reach. Then he notices his quarry is not silver but bronze, and then comes the final blow when a telltale spotted tail breaks the water. Then comes a slew of profanity-laden tirades.

"It's just a blanking redfish!"

"I blanking hate redfish!"

"If I catch another blanking redfish I'm going to scream!"

For hardcore trout fanatics, these are trying times. But for those of us who hold reds in high regard, they are times of pure joy.

Accidental encounters are common, but it is possible to target redfish with topwater lures. It just takes a little focus, willingness to try something different, and a heart strong enough to withstand intense excitement. The first thing to consider is where to fish. This might seem obvious, but the fact is some anglers just go to areas frequented by reds and assume they will have luck with topwaters. That is not the case.

The key to catching reds on topwaters is to be able to see them or at least locate signs of their feeding. Deep oyster reefs, for example, hold plenty of reds, but hooking one on a topwater there is not going to happen, at least not with any frequency.

I cut my teeth pursuing topwater reds in shallow marshes along the Upper Texas Coast, where I threw directly to the fish I wanted to catch. I could selectively target a big 30-inch brute or a barely legal sized 20-incher for the frying pan. It was truly a beautiful thing. My first successful outing was in a place called the "Twin Lakes" in Bridge City. Now part of the Lower Neches Wildlife Management Area, it serves as an intake reservoir for an Entergy Power Plant. The spot we scored on was a shallow flat that bordered two small islands in the marsh. The water in this spot was always super clear, so finding reds there was not a difficult task. The hardest part was not spooking them, so my father and I devised a shrewd game plan. We would come from the backside of the island by boat, anchor, and then walk across the island and fish from the bank. I have used this technique in other places, such as East Galveston Bay and Lake Calcasieu, where I found similar shallow, clear flats that held redfish.

Another good location for topwater reds is along shorelines in 2 to 3 feet of water. This sometimes requires a little closer observation than on the super shallow flats because the reds are not always visible. A telltale sign of redfish in these spots is mud boils spawned by the fish foraging around for crabs. Capt. Guy Schultz, who operates on Galveston Bay, is an Apache helicopter pilot for the Army reserve. He said while flying over that bay system he has seen trails of mud boils stretching for miles. From high up, these are easy to locate, but on the water they are not so easy to find.

If you are in a shallow area that you know reds school in, simply look for changes in water clarity. Fish the edges of the clear and murky and there is a good chance you will find redfish. Sometimes big schools of reds are responsible for screwing up water quality, so do not be afraid to give these spots a try.

An overlooked but excellent spot to catch reds on topwaters is along the weir systems that are common in Louisiana, and becoming more common in Texas. Reds in these locations feed on the shrimp, crab, and other creatures that dwell near the top of the

CCA Texas Director, Pat Murray, shows a nice redfish caught on a walker.

weir, and so they feed close to the surface. It is not unusual to see the reds surface feeding in these areas. Sub-surface lures are more popular for fishing these spots, but topwaters get the job done and then some.

I have caught Louisiana limits (five fish) of big reds on topwaters in the Cameron Prairie National Wildlife Refuge on the eastern side of Lake Calcasieu, and at Burton's Ditch, just five minutes from my home on the Louisiana side of the Sabine River.

Dan Olfatz of Alabama told me he catches reds on topwaters during high tides in tidal pools along the beaches in Alabama and Florida. He said the reds gather in the pools to feed on crab and will hit virtually anything you throw at them. My only experience catching reds on topwaters in the surf was the time I spotted some feeding along the rocks at Constance Beach in southwest Louisiana. I simply cast parallel to the rocks and yanked out redfish after redfish.

Something I learned early on was that redfish would only hit a lure put in front of them or directly to their side. They would never detect splashing behind them and turn around to investigate.

Later on, Ed Holder taught me about the red's "cone of vision." He said you have a 180-degree area from one eye, across the nose, and to the other eye to throw in and stay in the fish's sight. He said the best spot to cast is a few feet right in front of the red. They like to make a direct attack.

Many anglers, particularly on the Lower Texas Coast, talk about sight-casting to "tailing" redfish. What they mean is the reds are feeding in the shallows and their tails are sticking out of the water. In my region, we rarely saw "tailing" reds, but lots of "finning" ones. In other words, their backs and dorsal fin would stick out of the water. Finding "tailing" reds is quite exciting, however, and can give the angler a good sense of where to cast. If the

Watching a redfish take a topwater in the shallows makes for heart-pounding excitement.

TEXAS FISH & GAME

tail is facing one way, then the head will be in the opposite direction. This might seem obvious, but in the excitement of the
moment, such things are sometimes hard to remember. While
wade-fishing in the Chandeleur Islands back in the summer of 2000,
I came across a bunch of reds tailing. I was so excited at what I had
found that I cast directly past their tails. While walking my Top Dog
toward the fish, I realized the tail was facing me and their head was

going the other direction. That one still embarrasses me.

Gearing up for topwater redfishing requires no great preparation, but there are a few things to consider for optimum angling. A medium-heavy casting rod is ideal, and I prefer them a little on the heavy side. Reds are not particularly difficult to hook, but I make long casts with surface plugs, so I prefer a rod with backbone to help get a good hookset. After 24 years of fishing on the Gulf Coast, I am still amazed that a fish could hit a topwater plug armed with three treble hooks and not get stuck. To maximize hookset on reds, I have experimented with braided and fusion line (super line) and have had mixed results. The hookset advantage over monofilament is undeniable since super lines feature no-stretch properties. The problem comes with fighting the fish close to the boat. I have had several big reds make sudden, jerky runs right at the boat and break off. This is not a problem with monofilament.

My favorite monofilament is Berkley Big Game, but Stren Sensor is also good, along with Triple Fish and Excalibur. Nowadays, it is hard to go wrong with monofilament. If you choose to use braid for redfish, back off the drag a little once the fish gets close to the boat. If the fish starts to get away from you, it will be easy to readjust.

As far as plugs go, reds are not very fussy. In the lure chapter, I list a variety of topwaters and matching colors that I have field tested and found effective. The lure we used on my early outings in the "Twin Lakes" was the Jumpin' Minnow in bone color. If walked quickly, the reds would follow the plug, but rarely strike. When we slowed the presentation, watch out; a strike was inevitable.

My personal favorite topwaters for reds are walkers like the Top Dog, She Dog, Super Spook, and others. Some anglers call the Jumpin' Minnow a walker, but I do not really see it that way. They do walk, not in the same way as a Ghost or Top Dog. I especially like the Skitter Walk because it is by far the easiest to walk of any topwater I have ever fished—and I mean all of them. I discovered the lure while fishing in the Chandeleur Islands with Keith Warren and could not believe how simple it was to walk. That made it easy to fish and easy on my wrist after a hard day of fishing.

Despite what some anglers might tell you, there is no magic to walking a lure for reds other than the lure should twitch back and forth in a fluid motion. On the other hand, chuggers are effective and are great for making lots of noise and erratic motion. I have found chuggers like the Rattlin' Chug Bug and Pop-R great for catching reds in murkier water. I fish them more aggressively and drive my friends crazy with all of the noise I make. When the water is murky, I believe we need to give the fish all of the indicators we can so they can find and hit our plugs. "Wild" Bill Skinner of Bass-N-Mexico sold me on this when he came to Texas to seek redfish with me. The water was off-colored so he went to his tackle box and broke out some chuggers he designed himself. He caught plenty of reds and got me to rethink the use of chuggers for the species.

Speaking of hitting our plugs, it really is a miracle that redfish can hit anything on the surface. God designed them to feed on bottom-dwelling crustaceans, so they have to turn over or at least on their side to hit a topwater. Perhaps the reason they hit plugs with such gusto is they figure if they are going through the trouble of turning over to hit the thing, they might as well destroy it. That is why I love catching reds on topwaters so much. Outside of gator wrestling, it is the most intense thing going in Texas and Louisiana bay systems—and it's a tad bit safer. Well, it is for the angler. The plugs themselves do not have much of a life expectancy.

Big redfish like these caught in Louisiana are becoming more common on the Gulf Coast.

Multiple spots on this redfish make it almost as pretty as the lady holding it is. Almost.

Calm, slick summer days mean great redfish action on the open bays.

Scott Wyatt, caught this monster redfish, his first ever, while fishing with the author at the Sabine Jetties.

Rat-L-Traps are great lures for redfish.

Redfish have a funny habit of not liking anglers landing them. That might have something to do with a fillet knife and skillet of grease.

A big redfish can put smiles on the faces of the biggest of fellows.

Shakespeare's Mark Davis puts the companies surf rods to the test with this big Matagorda Island bull.

Multi-spotted redfish are common on the coast, but specimens like this one are not.

Joey James battles a big redfish on light tackle.

Capt. Skip James may look goofy in this Huckleberry-Finn style hat, but such contraptions do help beat the heat.

A nice cool fall day and stringer of redfish. Enough said.

Chapter
Four

Redfish School

I could not believe my eyes.

An acre-wide patch of water southwest of the Galveston Jetties churned and boiled with great fury. For a moment it seemed as if a nuclear submarine was surfacing, concern for national security eased when I saw mullet scurrying in the bronze-tinged mass of water, trying to avoid violent death by a massive school of bull red-fish—and I do mean massive. My jaw dropped and heart pounded at what I was witnessing. This was an angler's dream and I was experiencing it in vivid, living color.

Realizing that schooling reds do not stay on the surface for long, I grabbed a rod rigged with a Storm Rattlin' Chug Bug and fired it toward the fracas. Before I could pop the lure, a monster red hammered it and shot out of the water like a bronze rocket. Redfish rarely go airborne, but when they do it is a remarkable sight. The battle took more than 15 minutes, and by that time, the school dis-

Schooling redfish cause commotion unlike any other inland species.

appeared. I was elated, though, as 39 inches of measuring tape stretched from the red's nose to its tail. I knew there were bigger redfish in the school, but having caught a 39-incher on a topwater plug was a more than adequate consolation prize.

Beginning in mid-summer and lasting through the first couple of strong cold fronts in the fall, encounters like this are accessible to coastal anglers. In fact, with redfish numbers at the highest levels in recorded history, Texas Parks & Wildlife Department (TPWD) officials say such encounters are becoming increasingly common.

Redfish begin to school *en masse* in Texas bays during calm, slick days in late June. Most anglers never find them because they are running back to the boat ramp when the feeding action begins.

For some unknown reason, reds like to feed during the middle of the day when the temperatures soar and the bays are calm. Locating these fish requires glassing the bay and looking for water boiling and more subtle signs, like mysterious wakes and muddy patches surrounded by clear water. The key to successfully fishing these schools is to approach quietly. If you run up close and then throw over your trolling motor, you can forget it. These reds, despite their voracious nature, are very spooky. It is best to run up to them slowly, drop the trolling motor a hundred yards away, and ease in, or simply drift through them. I usually drift once I get close because even a trolling motor can put them down.

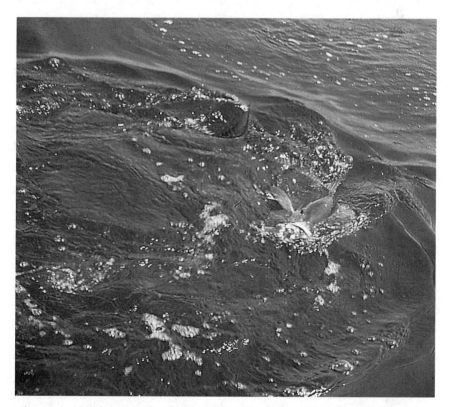

Churning and boiling water laced with a slight of bronze, or, like in this case a spotted tail sticking out of the water, is a sure sign redfish are schooling in an area.

The beautiful thing about these reds is they will hit virtually anything. Live shrimp, croaker, mullet, spoons, Rat-L-Traps, and soft plastics work just fine.

Sometimes, however, they are not so easy to locate and catch. Sabine Lake guide Capt. Skip James said school reds sometimes feed the outside edges of speckled trout schools instead of on the surface. During mid-summer, if you pick up a couple of reds in a school of trout, there are probably a bunch more lurking in the area.

"For a guy who's looking to bag some big reds and maybe has already caught his trout or would rather try something different, look to the outside of trout schools," James said. "Game fish feed in four distinct phases: packing, corralling, ambush, and mop-up. Packing involves the fish coming together to terrorize the baitfish population. This usually happens early on." It's during the next phase, corralling, that we start to notice some action, like nervous menhaden, scurrying shrimp and jumping ladyfish. During the ambush period, the feeding reaches a feverish frenzy, as the fish turn from passive to highly aggressive. This is the phase that the birds work and it is when you want to have your bait in the water.

"To catch schooling reds, I recommend a Rat-L-Trap or a big heavy spoon. Use something that you can chunk out there and reach the fish with, and that can get down toward the bottom fast. Additionally, have a few extra guns ready to shoot with. If you catch the fish on the feed, do not bother to unhook your fish if it is a legal one. Just lay it down for a second and fire another shot. It's important to maximize your time during the feeding frenzy."

James said that when targeting reds, it is crucial to avoid the small trout. He recommends backing off of a school if you catch a couple of small trout. They will get your bait before the reds do, so leave them be: "If I go in and catch a couple of little trout right off of the bat, I circle where I think the school is and try to find the reds. Often they will be on the outer edges of the trout, but you may have to search a little to find them."

The final stage of feeding phase is mop-up. This occurs after the main feeding is over and the fish seemingly get lockjaw. This is a great time to move into an area where trout have been schooling to locate reds. More often than not, they will move in on the remnants of a baitfish school and start biting when the trout leave.

"When the main bite is over, I will switch over from a Rat-L-Trap or spoon to a shrimp tail or Cocahoe Minnow and bounce it along the bottom, trying to rattle any roving reds attention. Glow and chartreuse are the best colors," James said.

James believes a common mistake is to leave an area during the mop-up period. The best bet is to set the trolling motor on low and cruise the perimeter, making 45-degree fan casts so that you can cover every angle. Think of redfish as scavengers waiting to attack the remnants of the trout's prey.

As summer wears on, action picks up in the nearshore Gulf of Mexico. Galveston guide Capt. Jim Leavelle said anglers can find monstrous schools of redfish from a few hundred yards from the surf on out to a couple of miles: "It's one of the most beautiful things you will ever encounter on the Texas coast. We have captured this phenomenon on video and people are always amazed at what they see."

These schooling reds will do one of two things: totally ignore your efforts or hit just about anything thrown at them. "Sometimes these reds can be spooky, so you have to be careful in approaching them," Leavelle said.

He is right. They may seem fearless as they madly thrash the water's surface, but they are actually a very cautious fish. In fact, I have found them to be twice as cautious as the smaller reds in the bay, and that may be an understatement. Follow the protocol for the schools in the bay, but remember this: If they disappear, approach the area where you last saw them and begin drifting. Sometimes they will follow the current to catch up with whatever they have been feeding on, so drifting is a good way to find them without making noise. Starting up the big motor is a no-no.

I have caught these reds on topwaters, Rat-L-Traps, and spoons, but by far the all-around best bait is a live croaker. I have never thrown a croaker into one of these schools that did not get gobbled up in short order. Big, bull redfish cannot resist live croaker, especially when they are in a feeding frenzy. The chances of catching them on lures is about 30 percent in my estimation, while using live croaker makes it virtually a done deal.

Something I noticed during one of my early encounters with Gulf schooling reds is the lack of gulls around them. The school that brought this to my attention was a few miles off the beach with no birds working, while just a couple of miles north, schools of small speckled trout drew in plenty of bird action. This has spawned debate among anglers who see it. One school of thought is the reds are targeting the Gulf menhaden. Still other anglers have said the reds are chasing large mullet and the gulls would rather pick off small shad and shrimp kicked up by the trout instead of gulping down a big baitfish. That was my assumption since I could see pods of mullet around the school, but the plot thickened when I cleaned a trio of these Texas slot-sized reds. (Most of these schooling reds are over the legal size limit and I release them to fight another day.) Two of them had empty stomachs while the other was stuffed with cutlass fish. These fish were all caught around 11 a.m. and it could be they had not fed since the previous day. All of the visible school-ing action was during the mid-day slick offs. Empty stomachs could indicate these reds might be feeding on whatever they can kill for a few hours and not feed until around the same time the next day. The ones we caught might have just started feeding.

I would like to learn more about this to see if there is a dis-cernable pattern to the behavior besides feeding during the mid-day period. The more I learn about them, the more I can catch.

Moving on to fall, anglers can find less mysterious schools of reds that come out of the marshes on the Upper Texas Coast. These fish are easy to find and catch. Besides the splishing, splashing, and gulping sounds of feeding predatory fish, there are other obvious visual indicators—the shallow water they inhabit often takes on a bronze tint.

Jack's Pocket in Trinity Bay is routinely one of the best spots to seek schooling reds in the fall; it may be the best spot on the entire Texas coast. The easiest way to find these frenzy-feeding schools is by locating diving gulls picking off the nervous baitfish pushed to the surface. Nevertheless, do not rely solely on birds to find the fish. On one trip to Jack's Pocket, my partner and I fished successfully for quite awhile without a single bird in view. Look for mud trails in the water, which often indicate redfish feeding.

Anglers typically throw spoons or soft plastic lures for these reds. I have used 12-pound test and a 3/8- to 1/2-ounce jighead to get past the small trout that often hang around the reds. The little specks feed on top as the reds are roving around the bottom. As Skip James recommended, fish down low to get the biggest and best fish.

Remember to drift over these schools rather than to fish them with a trolling motor. Once, a man fishing a school nearby me using his trolling motor only caught a few fish, while we had all the action we could handle. My friends and I watched him and he was pursuing the fish too aggressively. You can catch fish that way, but I believe it is possible to catch far more the way we did it. These big schools can provide the kind of action few coastal anglers get to experience, so pay attention to the details.

As observed earlier, I have been fortunate enough to encounter red schools on several occasions and have made a list of words that accurately describe this kind of fishing: exciting, fantastic, cool, phenomenal, fun.

You have to love that.

I know I do.

Chapter Five

Natural Bait:
Ain't nothing like the real thing, baby

Let's see, how does that song go...

..."ain't nothing like the real thing baby...."

I hate that song, but it drives home an important point for anglers serious about taking redfish: while artificial lures are highly effective, natural bait catches more fish.

Reds have voracious appetites and take to a variety of natural baits more quickly than other inshore species. I say "natural" baits because, with reds, it does not really matter whether the bait is live or dead; they are eclectic eaters.

Let's look at what baits are the most effective and how to properly use them.

BLUE CRAB

Blue crab is the best overall redfish bait there is. Nature designed reds to feed on crab, outfitting them with a downward pointing mouth, which is highly effective for preying on bottom-dwelling crustaceans. Anglers typically pull the shell off the crab, split the body down the middle, and hook it through the carapace. (The carapace is the back leg that looks like a paddle.) When fishing for bull reds, most anglers prefer using the whole crab, once again, with the top popped off.

Live crab are also effective for reds, especially when fished around nearshore oil and gas platforms in the Gulf of Mexico. Hook

them through the carapace and remove the claws for safer handling.

A few years ago, I met a man who used soft shell crab for bull redfish during the fall run. While I am sure it works, I consider that a crime against humanity. Soft shell crab is my all-time favorite seafood and I cannot fathom using it for bait when I could put it in

God designed redfish to eat crabs. The author believes he is too, but he is not proficient enough to catch them with his mouth yet.

Croaker may be a better bait than blue crab for redfish, especially the big redfish.

the frying pan and have an awesome meal. Catching redfish is great, but there is a point where I draw the line.

CROAKER

If I go out to specifically catch big reds, I always bring live croaker along. I have found it incredibly effective for drawing the strike of oversized reds in particular. I first discovered this while fishing at the Sabine Jetties after having sheepshead pick away the crab I was using. On my small rod, I caught an 8-inch croaker, hooked it through the lips, and tossed it out with one of my big rods. A few minutes later, it doubled over and I was battling a 42-inch bull red. During the course of the day, I caught nearly a dozen reds on live croaker, all of them oversized.

Back in 1999, fishing travel agent "Wild" Bill Skinner came over from New Mexico to catch bull redfish. We went out to the Sabine Jetties and fished with light action spinning rods to catch croaker for bait. Skinner caught the first one, which was a foot long and started to cut it in half for bait. He looked at me as if I were crazy when I told him we would use it whole and alive. I quickly snatched up the croaker, put it on a big Daiichi Tru-Turn hook, and threw it overboard. Remember, this croaker was a foot long. A few minutes later, Skinner was battling a monstrous redfish that measured 43 inches.

Live shrimp can tempt just about any gamefish, including reds.

This story illustrates my point about live bait, particularly croaker for redfish: the bigger the bait, the bigger the fish.

Hook croaker through the mouth or tail for best action.

SHRIMP

Live shrimp are great redfish bait. They stay lively in livewells and active on a hook, plus they are a top prey item for reds during fall. The only drawback to shrimp is that virtually everything in the bay eats them, making them difficult to keep on the hook for long in redfish territory. Frozen shrimp is the most accessible bait around and is effective for redfish.

MULLET

Mullet is a popular redfish bait that is usually fished dead and cut. It is popular with surf fishermen targeting bull reds since mullet are easy to catch with cast nets. Live mullet is also good and, like croaker, the rule is to use big bait to catch big fish. If you are tar-

Mud minnows may seem like flounder bait, but redfish will not turn them down.

geting reds within the Texas slot limit, use smaller mullet. If you want a beast, do not be afraid to use mullet big enough to put in the frying pan.

MENHADEN

Menhaden, also known as pogies or shad, are another good choice. Moreover, like most redfish baits, they are effective both alive and dead. During late summer and fall, live menhaden fished under a popping cork on the main body of a bay is a killer method, especially when using an Alameda Rattler or a similar rattling cork rig. The ideal size is 3 to 4 inches long.

Keeping these delicate fish alive is a difficult task that I have only been able to do by using pure oxygen or an expensive recycling aeration system. They die quickly in hot weather.

A new trend among coastal anglers is fishing with "cold shad." This technique involves catching them by cast net and immediately putting them on a layer of ice and then covering them with another layer. Make sure to drain as much water out as possible to keep the shad fresh. Fish them just as you would the live version.

MUD MINNOW (GULF KILLIFISH, COCAHOE)

Mud minnows are underrated redfish bait. As detailed in my book, *Texas Trout Tactics*, several years ago while flounder fishing I decided to use some leftover mud minnows for speckled trout, and it worked. What I did not mention in that book is that we also caught many redfish that day.

While drifting a large oyster reef, my father and I fished with live mud minnows under popping corks. We caught a two-man limit of redfish on a reef that was 12 feet deep. We rigged our minnows to suspend about halfway down.

Cast nets are an indispensable tool for live bait fishermen.

The main advantage to using mud minnows is they are a hardy fish that anglers can hook several ways: through both lips, behind the dorsal (top) fin, or through the body near the tail.

SAND TROUT

Sometimes when jetty fishing, croaker can be difficult to find, but sand trout are easy to catch. I have had good luck using both cut and live sand trout for reds. Sand trout stays on the hook well, too, but it is very appealing to sharks and stingrays. That does not bother me a bit, but for some anglers it is a little unnerving.

FIDDLER CRAB

These tiny crab are hard to catch, but make excellent redfish bait, especially when fished in shallow salt marshes where they are common. Give them a chance if you cannot catch anything else.

PIGGY PERCH, PINFISH

These baitfishes are far more effective for catching speckled trout than redfish, but they do work from time to time. My advice would be to use them only as a last resort.

CRAWFISH

Redfish stocked in freshwater areas feed heavily on crawfish, and although it may seem a bit unorthodox, it works well in coastal marshes as well. Hook the crawfish through the tail so it stays alive.

CATCHING BAIT

A cast net is an indispensable tool for anglers serious about catching bait for redfish. I have been throwing a cast net since I was eight years old, and have always found it lots of fun. To this day, I take pride in catching my own bait.

Cast nets are great for catching mullet, menhaden, and shrimp, and can save thousands of dollars over a lifetime of fishing. If you are on a budget, learn to use a cast net because buying bait from a marina is expensive.

A tip for anglers new to using cast nets is to not use one that is too big. There is no shame in using a 6-foot net while others around you are using 12- and 14-footers. It does you no good to use a huge net if you cannot throw it correctly. Accuracy in casting can make up for width of a net.

Cast nets cannot catch all baitfishes effectively, and crab are a prime example. The best way to get crab is to buy a crab trap and set it out the night before you go fishing. You can purchase traps for about $30 at commercial fishing supply stores. They are an invaluable tool for anglers serious about using crab.

Mud minnows are caught mostly in traps, which sell for about half of what a good crab trap costs. Mud minnow traps can be set along shallow ditches in the marsh or near the bay and are

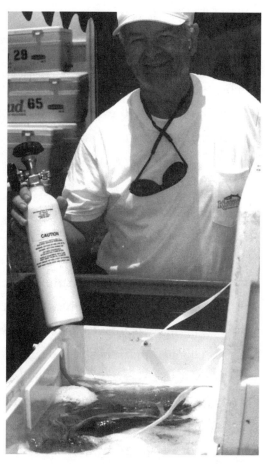

Wanna keep bait alive? If so, David Kinser shows how he does it with an oxygen bottle. Putting pure oxygen into the water is essential to keeping baitfish kicking.

extremely efficient. Perch traps, which are available at commercial fishing outlets and some bait shops, are good for catching piggy perch, pinfish, and croaker.

I have found it is best to use rod and reel to catch croaker. I like to use (the really big ones). I usually use croaker while jetty fishing, so I bring along a light action-spinning rod rigged with a double leader and baited with dead shrimp. If there are croaker in the area, it does not take long to find them, then when I put the croaker on as bait, it does not take redfish long to find *them*.

Sand trout, as noted earlier, are a good substitute for croaker and anglers can catch them the same way. The only difference is I catch larger sand trout on cut bait rather than shrimp. I recommend a treble hook for sand trout, but cut bait is a magnet for hardheads and there is nothing more annoying than having to remove a treble hook from these dangerous-to-handle fish.

KEEPING BAIT ALIVE

As detailed in *Texas Trout Tactics*, the secret to using live bait is simple: keep it alive. Well, the concept may be simple, but actually keeping some baitfishes breathing can be a challenge.

For bank fishermen, a large Styrofoam ice chest will do a good job keeping most baitfishes kicking. Styrofoam breathes and if the water is changed periodically, most bait will do well.

For anglers in boats, a recirculating livewell is the ideal setup. By exchanging water frequently, anglers can achieve low bait mortality in many situations. A great aid to keeping bait alive is chemical additives produced by Sure-Life Laboratories. They have chemicals out called Pogy-Saver, Croaker-Saver, Shrimp-Saver, and stuff designed specially for mullet and many other baitfishes. A couple of spoonfuls of this stuff will help eliminate ammonia in the water, a byproduct produced naturally by the baitfishes themselves which accumulates and kills them.

Unbelievably, some anglers use sawdust to keep shrimp alive. Back in the 1970's and early 1980's, some bait camps sold live shrimp in sawdust. Some, particularly in Florida, still carry on this tradition. Sawdust holds in moisture and actually keeps the shrimp alive longer than just sitting in a regular bait bucket. The strange thing is that it is very important not to dampen the sawdust too

Aerators are the standard way of caring for baitfish.

much. It will kill the shrimp.

A similar technique involves an ordinary towel. Bring along a towel and wet it with the water the shrimp came from. Then fold the towel in half and place it in your cooler. After that, lift the top layer of the towel and put the shrimp all over the towel in a single layer. Then fold it back down so it covers the shrimp.

This will cause the shrimp to look dead, but they are really in a state of suspended animation and can live for up to 24 hours. As soon as you hook the shrimp and put it in the water, it will come alive.

If you are dead set on keeping bait alive you need to use pure, dissolved oxygen. I have been a proponent of David Kinser's Oxygen Edge system for years. It is the best investment I have ever made for live bait fishing. Having had an Oxygen Edge Unit since early 1998, I can attest to its absolute effectiveness. Speaking very conservatively, it has reduced live bait mortality in my live well by 80 percent.

Instead of relying on standard aeration to keep bait or tournament fish alive, Kinser's system involves super-charging the water with pure oxygen.

"Standard aeration systems draw from the air, which is composed of 21 percent oxygen." Kinser said. "Factor in that many units only achieve 65 to 80 percent efficiency, and it becomes obvious what happens when water temperatures start to heat up. The fish start to die because they are not getting enough oxygen."

Another advantage of using the Edge is that it keeps baitfish "super-charged." The oxygen keeps their metabolism so high that they are very frisky and more likely to attract a response from a game fish.

According to the Bait Care Company, when shad are held in bait buckets, they are usually very crowded. This results in physical abrasion, poisonous ammonia build-up, and short-lived bait. They say to keep shad healthy, add Shad Protector as soon as the fish go in the bucket. Keep the bait bucket out of the sun. Cooler water holds more oxygen and makes it easier for the fish to breathe. If the water in the bait bucket looks dirty, change half of the water and add another dose of Shad Protector. Repeat this procedure throughout the day as necessary. When keeping shad in a bucket for an extended time, a battery-powered aerator is recommended to maintain an adequate oxygen level.

Chapter Six

The Artificial Approach

Some of the first lures designed specifically for saltwater were produced to target redfish. Back in the 1950's, anglers began throwing gold spoons at reds on the coast and found the fish responded favorably to these simple chunks of metal. A few years later, a few soft plastic lures designed for reds hit the market, with early models closely resembling crude bass worms.

When I was a kid, we rarely used lures for redfish, but the store we stopped at before going fishing had a small lure rack stocked with a locally made "redfish lure," which was a 6-inch, pink plastic worm with a white jighead and another hook rigged toward the tail. This thing fascinated me, so one day Dad bought me one to try. I never caught a red on it, but I sure had fun fishing with it.

Nowadays, there are hundreds of lures made for redfish and they are all fun to fish. There is just something about a red hitting a lure that makes me want to go fishing.

Enough with the remembrances, let's look at some good redfish lures.

LURE: JOHNSON SPOON

Best Season(s): Year-round

Color: Gold or Bronze

Application/location:
Throw to areas where reds
are visibly attacking baitfishes, or work along drop-offs
and in grassy areas. When
reds are schooling, this is a
good lure to throw because
you can get distance on it
and not spook the fish.

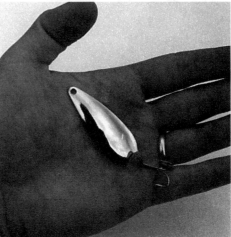

Technique: Chuck it
out, reel it in with a varying

Johnson Spoon

retrieve. When fishing jetties
or deep holes, chunk it out and let it flutter.

Tips: If you are serious about catching redfish, this is a must-
have. There is no better redfish lure.

LURE: SPIVEY SCENT TRAIL SPOON

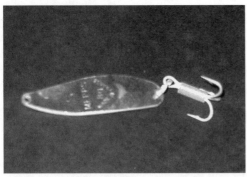

Spivey Scent Trail Spoon

Best Season(s):
Year-round

Color: Gold

Application/location:
My first test of this thing
was in the Intracoastal
Canal near East Galveston
Bay. Some redfish were

working along a shallow flat. After spraying down a gold edition of this spoon with scent and ripping it through the flat, I caught my Texas limit of legal-sized fish plus a few "rat reds." I intentionally threw the spoon upcurrent of the reds to see if they would get hold of the scent, and to my surprise, it seemed to have some effect on them. One of the reds swam about 15 feet up the flat to get to the spoon, which I was dragging slowly across the bottom. This could have been from hearing the splash of it hitting the water, or the scent might have turned the fish on. Either way, I caught the fish.

Technique: Chuck it out, reel in with a varying retrieve. In the winter, this is a good one to walk slowly along the bottom, letting the scent trail lure reds to the spoon.

Tips: Do not spray too much of the juice on the absorbent strip. On my first cast, I sprayed three times and created an Exxon Valdez-class oil slick. One spray is plenty; the "Dyn-O-Scent" goes a long way

LURE: RIP TIDE WEEDLESS SHRIMP

Best Season(s): Summer, Fall

Color: Smoke, Red Mist, Pearl, Glow, Chartreuse

Application/location: Since it is weedless, this is a good lure to fish in the marsh during the high tides that often come in later summer and early fall.

Technique: Throw around clumps of grass in

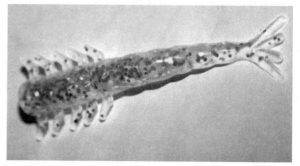

Rip Tide Weedless Shrimp

marsh and in areas with heavy vegetation. Aim for specific areas and work over heavily.

Tips: Do not be afraid to drag through heavy grass. The lure makers designed it for fishing in the grass.

Lure: D.O.A. Crab

Best Season(s): Winter

Color: Brown, Root Beer, Chartreuse

Application/location: God made reds to feed on crabs. Fish this bait in marshes or anywhere else crab congregate.

Technique: Drag very, very slowly across the bottom.

D.O.A. Crab

Tips: Not to beat a dead horse, but as D.O.A. lure maker Mark Nichols says, fish it "slower than evolution."

Lure: Catch-Em Lures Sabine Snake

Best Season (s): Spring

Color: Fire Tiger, June bug, Chartreuse

Application/location: This lure is designed to imitate sand eels and is best fished on oyster reefs in spring where many redfish hang out. It is also good in the marsh.

Technique: Fish this one on a breakaway rig or bounce on a hefty jighead when fishing on reefs. In the marsh, use a Texas rig as you would for largemouth, or simply rig on a 1/4-ounce jighead.

Tips: Work this lure with a fast retrieve. Eels move fast, so it will look natural.

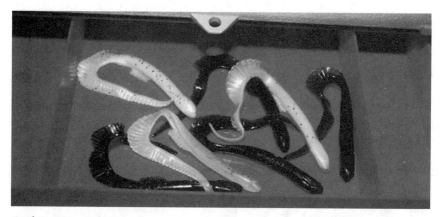

Catch-Em Lures Sabine Snake

LURE: CHUG BUG

Best Season(s): Spring, Summer, Fall

Color: Various

Application/location: This lure is excellent for catching schooling reds in the late summer and fall.

Technique: As the name implies, this lure is a "chugger." Use a quick twitch of the rod tip to make the dished-out face *Chug Bug* "chug" and throw spray.

Tips: Do not try to walk it, chug it.

LURE: TWISTER TAIL

Color: White, Chartreuse, Glow

Best Season(s): Year-round

Application/location: This lure is best fished on a 1/8- or 1/4-

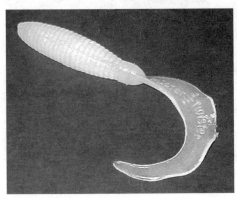

ounce jighead around the mouth of marsh points and along the shorelines of bay systems. This is not a good lure to fish in heavy current.

Technique: Drag slowly across the bottom or moderately hop it up and down.

Tips: There is another version of this lure called the

Zap Twister Tail

Spin Top combo that has a slightly different jighead and a small teardrop-bladed spinner fitted on it. It is hard to find, but an excellent lure.

MirrOlure Top Dog

LURE: MIRROLURE TOP DOG

Color: Bone, Black, Chartreuse.

Best Season(s): Spring, Summer, Fall

Application/location: Fish this one anywhere you think a top-water explosion could happen.

Technique: Walk the dog, plain and simple.

Tips: The Top Dog is one of the most popular lures of all time, and for good reason. It is easy to walk, cast, and catch fish on. I like to use this with braided line. I find the lure walks better and the braided line increases my hook-to-land ratio.

LURE: NORTON SAND EEL

Best Season(s): Spring

Color: Glow/Chartreuse, Pearl, Red Shad

Application/location: This lure is a fine imitator of the sand eel, which is a chief prey item of reds in the early spring. It can catch reds anywhere, but is best fished over oyster reefs.

Technique: I have found this lure to be effective when fished on a 3/8-ounce jighead and bounced on the bottom.

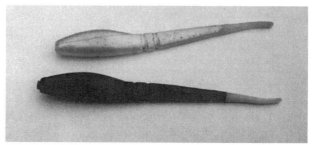

Norton Sand Eel

Tips: This lure, unlike the Sabine Snake, should not be fished with a fast retrieve. It moves quickly through the water on its own in areas of strong current.

LURE: RAT-L-TRAP

Best Season(s): Year-round

Color: Chrome and Black, Chrome and Blue

Application/location: Open bays, shorelines, cuts, and offshore

around oil rigs

Technique: Most anglers are familiar with ripping this lure through schools of reds or using it as a locator to work down shorelines and canals. A virtually unknown but highly effective method for the 'Trap involves letting it hit the bottom and slowly scooting it. This is killer during winter months when reds are more sluggish. Around oil rigs in the nearshore Gulf, throw it out, let flutter down around the platform legs, and reel up with a medium retrieve.

Tips: Use a shock leader to lessen the chances of losing these expensive lures.

LURE: PRODUCER GHOST

Best Season(s): Spring, Summer, Fall

Color: Bone

Application/location: Like the Top Dog, fish this one anywhere you think a topwater explosion could happen.

Technique: Walk the dog.

Tips: When a red first hits this lure, do not set the hook hastily. Let the fish take some line then make a hookset.

LURE: FAT FREE SHAD

Best Season(s): Summer, Fall

Color: Tennessee Shad Chrome

Application/location: Use this in ship channels to locate reds hanging in deep water, and at jetties.

Technique: Rip this one

Excalibur Fat Free Shad

through the water fast, or rip it fast in short bursts, let it suspend, and repeat.

Tips: This lure was designed for bass, but it is great for redfish.

LURE: H&H 1/2-OUNCE SPINNERBAIT

Best Season(s): Summer, fall

Color: White, Yellow, Chartreuse

Application/location: Yet another bass lure, this is a great one to fish in the marsh around grass lines and in the mouths of cuts.

Technique: Spinners are easy to fish. Simply slow-roll it or use a fast retrieve. I usually start with a slow roll, then go to a fast retrieve if the fish do not respond.

Tips: Do not feel goofy for using this on redfish; it works.

LURE: SASSY SHAD

Best Season(s): Spring, Summer, Fall

Color: Natural Shad, Pearl, Chartreuse

Application/location: In spring, use the smallest version of the lure to fish in eddies where small shad go to rest. During summer and fall, go to the big 5-inch to target reds feeding on larger menhaden.

Technique: Drag the lure slowly across the bottom or hop it up

Mister Twister Sassy Shad

and down.

Tips: Be mindful of size for the different seasons. You have to "match the hatch," so to speak. The rule of thumb is small in spring and larger in summer and fall.

LURE: ARBOGAST HULA POPPER

Color: Various

Best Season(s): Spring, Summer, Fall

Application/location: This old bass fishing lure is excellent for catching schooling in late summer and fall. I first learned of its effectiveness when fishing the marshes of Venice, Louisiana, where it is a popular redfish bait.

Technique: As the name implies, this lure is a "popper." Twitch the rod tip to make it pop and splash.

Tips: If you get "followers" that will not strike, stop the lure, stick your rod tip beneath the surface, then reel in very fast. The lure will dive beneath the surface and wobble through the water, leaving a trail of bubbles. This can elicit a "reaction strike."

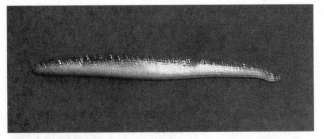

Rapala Shad Assassin

LURE: SHAD ASSASSIN

Color: Various

Best Season(s): Winter, Early Spring

Application/location: This is a slow-sinking plastic that anglers sometimes use without a jighead during winter.

Technique: Fish with a very slow retrieve.

Tips: Try this lure fished "wacky style." Hook the lure in the center and let it sink without a weight. It works great for bass, and I have caught quite a few reds and trout that way.

LURE: RAPALA SKITTER POP

Color: Various

Best Season(s): Summer, Fall

Application/location: Use anywhere you would normally use a topwater.

Technique: Pop slowly or skid the lure across the water.

Tips: Do not throw this lure out too far. Fish it fairly close to the boat for optimum action.

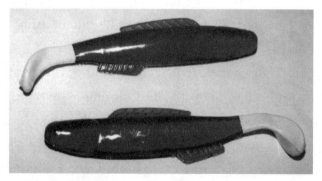

Berkley Power Mullet

LURE: BERKLEY POWER MULLET

Best Season(s): Summer, Fall

Color: Glow/Chartreuse, Purple/Yellow for murky conditions

Application/location: This is a good lure for fishing in river systems and marshes above bays, where reds are common.

Technique: This is a good lure to use on a fish-finder (Carolina) rig, and it is good to bounce on the bottom.

Tips: Bring a bunch. Reds tear up this one.

MODIFYING LURES

Many anglers are no longer relying on lure manufacturers to produce specific colors, shapes, and actions in lures. Many of them are adapting to conditions in the waters they fish to come up with some unusual and productive modifications.

A reader of my "Outdoors Page" in the *Port Arthur News* sent a very interesting topwater modification to me. He links three Rattlin' Chug Bugs together with 80-pound Spiderwire. The first lure is a Big Bug, the second is the standard Chug Bug, and the third is a Baby Bug. He said it imitates a school of baitfish. He simply pops or chugs the lure instead of walking the dog with it. Judging from the digital picture he sent of some of the fish he caught using this modification, I may try it myself this year.

Soft plastic lures are easy to modify and coastal anglers often experiment with them. Colorite Bait Coloring System produced by the Colorite Bait Company (colorite@flash.net) out of Alvin, Texas, makes modifications easy. One of my favorite colors for topwater is anything with a red head and white body. Once I got the Colorite system, I translated this over to plastics by taking a white shrimp tail and dipping the first half-inch in a red tail dip. This stuff dries quickly and stays with the lure, which makes it practical to carry along on a fishing trip for last minute modifications.

A bass angler from Kentucky sent me one of the neatest modifications I have seen, and I believe could be productive for redfish. When fishing a Texas rig for bass, he rigs up two worms instead of

This rack of plugs has been battered, beaten and abused.

one. He puts on a barrel swivel and then makes two one-foot leaders down to a worm hook and bullet weight, and then hooks on his worms. He claims this drives the bass crazy and has helped him to win several local fishing tournaments. I have considered using this for saltwater fishing with the Norton Sand Eel or Culprit Worm, both excellent lures for imitating the eels so common on Texas oyster reefs. I pour some of my own jigheads, so I have made jigheads with a double hook. I am going to fish the lures close together and see what happens. For anglers who do not have their own equipment for this, just use the Texas-rig method. It will produce about the same action as a jighead, and it might be fun to tell your friends you smoked the reds on a Texas-rigged worm. They may never believe you, but it does not matter if you catch fish.

The simple addition of a popping cork can give a lure an entirely different life. While drift-fishing over heavy grass or structure, it might pay to fish a Rat-L-Trap under a popping cork, especially during winter months when the fish's metabolism is slow. The movement of the current should keep the action going, and by using a cork, it is possible to stay away from tangles. In addition, the popping of the cork gives it a unique action.

Call me crazy, call me strange, but these modifications work. Sometimes fish do not like to cooperate, so we have to influence them a little. I say, when it comes to catching reds, the motto should be "by all means necessary." That includes the weird stuff.

TIPS FROM THE PROS

The next time you go for redfish, consider these tips from the experts at Pure Fishing.

1. A good angler hears and sees well and his or her mind instantly registers the impressions. If a redfish nails a baitfish on the surface behind you, your ears should convey the message. The trick is to train our senses to accept the commonplace sights and sounds in nature and seek out the unusual. Always be alert on the water.

2. Most anglers put life into a soft plastic lure by using the reel instead of the rod. That is entirely the wrong approach. Dragging a lure with the reel robs the lure of its built-in action. Instead, keep the rod tip high while using it to move the life-like piece of plastic. Lift the rod to move the lure, allow it to settle down to the bottom, and then reel in the excess slack.

4. One of the most deadly techniques for soft-plastic lures like jigs and grubs is vertical jigging. One way to trigger strikes from sluggish redfish is to cast a lure over a clump of grass, then jig the lure up and down several times. Finicky redfish will usually fall victim to this yo-yo motion.

5. Muddy water is not all bad. It does not mean that your chance of catching fish is over. It just means that you have to change your approach. Muddy water actually provides some advantages

because it positions redfish at a predictable depth. The fish are less spooky, and dark-water redfish are more likely to attack a lure invading their territory than those that can examine it in clear water. If the water is chocolate-colored, the fishing will suffer, but if it is a little off-colored, you may be in luck.

Chapter Seven

Stealth Techniques:
Fly-fishing, kayaks and clandestine wading

Catching a redfish with fly-fishing gear is almost too much fun for one person to stand. It is part of what I call "stealth techniques" that allow close contact with these spooky fish.

As noted in my previous book, *Texas Trout Tactics*, I am not a fly-fishing expert, but I do enjoy participating in the sport from time to time. In fact, while conducting in the field research for the book I caught my first ever redfish on a fly rod.

It was a classic setup. While wade-fishing along a piece of protected shoreline in East Galveston Bay, I cast a Clouser Minnow alongside a small pod of mullet. Before I could even work the bait, a big red engulfed it and locked me in a battle I will never forget. This thing ran up and down the shoreline as if it were crazy, and for a while I did not think the rod was going to hold up. Ten minutes later, I landed a beautiful, 24-inch, blue-tailed redfish that I consider one of my top angling trophies.

Fly-fishing is a delicate sport that can make for adrenaline-pumping action.

Catching this hefty fish on fly gear got me to wondering what is the best setup for saltwater fly-fishing, so I consulted the people at Orvis, who made the following recommendations:

Step 1: Find the proper line weight. Generally, the line weight determines the size of the fly you can accurately cast. Line weights come in sizes 1 through 14, with 1 the lightest. Most anglers use lighter lines for smaller fish in smaller water. Conversely, when fishing large rivers and saltwater, you would go to heavier lines to throw larger flies. Decide where and what you are fishing for, and choose a line in that category.

Step 2: Like line, rods come in various "weights" that must match the line weight. Beyond that, choose a rod length appropriate for the venue. Large rivers and saltwater offer you the opportunity to cast aggressively and use a longer rod. Longer rods also help greatly in situations where reaching and mending line are necessary. Saltwater anglers generally use 9- to 9-1/2-foot rods for big open water.

Step 3: Choose your flex. It is largely a matter of personal preference, but it is important. If you choose to use Orvis gear, a new technique called the Orvis Flex Index makes this choice easier than ever. After two years of work, Orvis engineers have developed a numerical method and a scale to quantify the flex pattern of each rod that Orvis manufactures. Every Orvis fly rod has its flex index stamped right on the rod along with the length and weight. It will soon become one of the most important factors in your search for the right fly rod.

According to Orvis, this process is very simple:

Let's say you have a 5-weight that you love dearly and think is the finest casting tool ever built. Now you need a 10-weight and you want the same familiar and comfortable action.

Before Flex Index was developed, it would have required a long and laborious quest, casting a number of rods, trying to find that one rod that casts like your 10-weight. With the new Orvis Flex Index, that problem is eliminated.

You can now walk to the rack and find the rod that is labeled with the identical or closest number on the flex scale to the rod you like. Its casting properties will be similar if not identical. Most anglers will not notice a difference in rod action unless the Flex Index varies by two points or more. This will hold true for any length and weight rod you decide you need.

Each Orvis rod can now be identified as a full flex, mid flex, or tip flex rod, and can be narrowed down even further within those designations to an absolute number.

PERSONAL CHOICES AND FLY PATTERNS

The way I see it, purchasing fly-fishing gear is another scenario where you get what you pay for. If you plan on trying this sport, you might want to get an inexpensive saltwater combo, but if you are really into it, more expensive gear is required. Not all fly-fishing tackle is equal, but if you are an expert, I do not need to tell you this; you could teach me a few things about the sport.

Nowadays, anglers have a huge variety of flies to choose from, many of which are as effective as they are colorful.

Clouser Minnow: Most saltwater fly-fishermen say if they had to choose only one fly for all their fishing, this would be it. It is great in the shallows and in deep water. I caught my first redfish on a chartreuse/white variation. I also caught my first speckled trout on it.

Half/Half: This shrimp imitation is a heavy sinking fly that requires a slow-to-fast action. This makes it resemble a shrimp's herky-jerky actions.

Muddler Minnow: Some call this the "all-time classic redfish fly." It resembles a minnows and is responsible for catching many redfish, particularly in Florida, where it is very popular.

Deceiver Menhaden: This is another popular fly, and one I have fished in No. 5/0 with a white and pink pattern.

Bay Anchovy: There are many of good patterns of small translucent baitfishes to choose. These are great because they come in many sizes and can help you "match the hatch." You can get these from 1/2-inch up to 3 inches long.

Lefty's Deceiver: This fly is named after fly-fishing legend Lefty Kreh, and often produces when others will not. It is very popular among fly-fishing enthusiasts, particularly in Florida.

Poppers: Poppers are fun to fish with because they are the top-water plugs of the fly-fishing world. Enough said.

PRESENTATION

Casting to reds means getting the fly close to the fish and into its "cone of vision," as discussed elsewhere in this book. The key is

Flyfishing expert Phil Shook pulls a kayak through marsh on the Gulf Coast somewhere. Kayaks are great for getting into areas otherwise inaccessible by motorboats.

casting close enough so that it sees the fly but does not spook. Lead the fish by 10 feet so that you can strip the fly to intersect its path.

When a redfish strikes your fly, use a firm, strip-strike when you feel the hit. Do not strike directly up the rod, because if the redfish has the fly, it may come shooting out of the water. Some anglers prefer a firm rod strike to the side. It is best to keep your rod tip high while forming a circle with your left forefinger and thumb to smoothly clear the line. Now you can concentrate on landing the fish. Keep the rod tip high so you can avoid getting the line snapped on underwater obstructions. This includes grass, which can easily accumulate on the line.

KAYAKS

A growing number of coastal anglers are using kayaks to maneuver in bay, lagoon, and surf systems. These lightweight crafts may look like something out of an Alaska wilderness film, but they are highly effective right here on the Gulf Coast, where the sand meets the surf.

Port O'Connor fishing guide Capt. Everett Johnson believes kayaks may very well be the wave of the future for coastal fishing: "Wade-fishing has been the thing for so long because of the stealth issue. People want to be quiet approaching big fish, so they understandably go to the technique they know is effective, but there are certain distinct advantages to using a kayak. Besides stealth, there are issues such as physical conditioning and access, which kayaks address."

Kayaks are sleek, quiet crafts that allow anglers to get literally right on top of fish without spooking them. According to Johnson: "Someone seated in a kayak can get closer to a redfish than by any other method I've tried. I've been within 10 feet of reds and had to sit motionless until they moved off a few yards before I dared reach for my rod. These craft have a very low profile and can be maneuvered without a sound. In clear waters, kayaks can be slowly cruised over areas while anglers look for fish, which isn't quite as easy to do when simply wading. You can't cover as much ground."

After publishing an article about kayak fishing last summer, I conducted a kayak stealth test (albeit very unscientific). My friend Bill Killian and I took out a fiberglass bass boat and a small kayak. I also took along scuba gear.

I dropped down to the bottom in five feet of water using the scuba gear, and got Bill to pass over my position in the fiberglass boat using a trolling motor. I could easily hear him passing overhead. Then he made a pass in the kayak. Although I could see the boat, I could barely hear him paddling. The next test was for Bill to wade in 3 feet of water on a sand bar a couple of hundred yards away while I rested on the bottom in scuba gear. I told him to move quietly as he would while wade-fishing. The results were the kayak was quieter than either the bass boat with trolling motor or wading. Actually, the trolling motor method was quieter than the wading.

Kayaking does not require athletic physical conditioning, according to Johnson: "I would say that any person in decent or average physical condition would make a good candidate to learn kayaking. If you like to mix in a little exercise with your fishing, then all the more reason to take up the paddle. If you are presently out of shape or restrained in some way, they are still plenty of fun. I always use the analogy of the bicycle, which is 'paddle or peddle at your own speed.' Actually, fishing out of a kayak is probably less strenuous than wading on mucky bottoms."

Another issue kayaks address is fishing access. Many coastal anglers do not own boats, and most of the time that is due to finances. A new bay boat can cost nearly $20,000, while a kayak can cost under $1,000. Sure, a bay boat will take an angler greater distances in a shorter time, but kayaks allow anglers to get into spots motor boats simply cannot go. It takes only a few inches of water for a kayak to remain afloat. Some of the best spots to kayak are tidal lakes, tidal flats, and remote salt marsh lakes.

The kayak can open a whole new world to the fisherman whose bay rig needs 1 to 2 feet of water to navigate safely and comfortably. Some of these salt marsh lakes are 6 inches deep in spots, but they hold many fish. Also, many of these areas are located a short distance from bank fishing spots, where a quick trip in a kayak could put the angler into area no one else can go. In the world of redfishing, that is a real plus.

Because kayaks are much smaller and lighter than other craft, they pose safety issue beyond those of other boaters. Here are some kayak safety tips from the Maine Island Trail Association, a group dedicated to safe kayaking and other outdoor activities.

ALWAYS TAKE:

- a kayak in good, serviceable condition, with plenty of secure buoyancy, fore and aft
- a paddle
- spray cover that fits your boat
- personal flotation device and whistle
- clothing suitable for all conditions
- bailer or pump
- accessible spare paddle, minimum 1 per group

Wade-fishing requires good gear and a willingness to stay in the water despite the presence of everything from stingrays to sharks.

In any but the most benign conditions, also consider:

- accessible flare pack
- flashlight (even for day trips)
- self-rescue aids
- rain gear and extra clothing in a waterproof bag
- minimum of 25 feet of towline
- charts and tide tables
- compass
- knife
- matches or a lighter
- first aid kit
- weather radio

PRECAUTIONS FOR BEGINNERS:

- familiarize yourself with your boat
- start gradually in moderate weather, close to shore, and with an experienced companion.
- develop your paddling skills, turning, and bracing
- carry safety equipment
- leave a float plan
- get a weather forecast before you go out each day
- know the principles of navigation and seamanship
- watch out for other watercraft and know right-of-way (a larger vessel always has the right-of-way)

WADE-FISHING

Sometimes, it simply pays to get in the water with the redfish. This is an especially good method when a falling tide reveals redfish actively feeding in the shallows with their tails or dorsal fins sticking out of the water. At these times, the fish can be caught by sight-casting.

While wading for reds, it is important to dress properly. Quality wade-fishing belts, like the Wade-Aid, provide superior back support and plenty of places to carry gear. Walking through water can tire muscles quickly and cause back pain in anglers even in the best of shape.

During winter months, neoprene waders are a must-have item. Catching redfish is cool and everything, but hypothermia is not—no pun intended. Wade-fishermen face other hazards. Rip currents are the most threatening natural hazard along our coast. They pull victims away from the beach. The United States Lifesaving Association has found that 80 percent of the rescues affected by ocean lifeguards involve saving those caught in rip currents.

A rip current is a seaward moving current that circulates water back to sea after the waves push it ashore. Each wave accumulates water on shore, creating seaward pressure. This pressure releases in an area with the least amount of resistance, which is usually the deepest point along the ocean floor. Rip currents also exist in areas where objects such as rock jetties, piers, natural reefs, and even large groups of bathers weaken the waves. Rip currents often look like muddy rivers flowing away from shore.

Rip currents are sometimes mistakenly called "rip tides" or "undertows." These are misnomers. Rip currents are not directly associated with tides and they do not pull people under.

Try to avoid wading where rip currents are present. If you become caught in one, swim parallel to the shore until the pull stops, and then swim back to shore. If you are unable to return to the beach, tread water, and try to attract the attention of your fishing partner—never wade-fish alone. Stay at least 100 feet away from piers and jetties; rip currents often exist along the side of fixed objects in the water.

Clearly, wade-fishing is not for everyone.

To those who have never seriously pursued wade-fishing, you may consider it strange to soak oneself in saltwater and face hazards like stingrays, when boats offer more comfort and the ability to cover more ground more quickly—but that is exactly what dedicated waders do not like.

From my standpoint, I see stealth as a very important aspect of wading. Because walking in saltwater can be flat out tough, wading forces the angler to fish slower and look at an area differently. Being in a more intimate relationship with your surroundings creates a different perspective, and sometimes that is what it takes to get anglers to see the little things that can lead to a limit.

Chapter Eight

Redfish Hotspots:

Anglers seeking redfish have no problem scoring virtually anywhere along the Gulf Coast. Conservation efforts directed at the species have enhanced the fishery to an astounding level, but that does not mean certain spots are not better than others are. Here are the best of the best.

JACK'S POCKET (TRINITY BAY)

It does not take a PhD to figure out where the redfish are in Trinity Bay during the fall. Besides the splashing and gulping sounds of feeding predatory fish, there are other obvious visual indicators—the water takes on a strange bronze tint.

Jack's Pocket in Trinity Bay is routinely one of the best spots to seek schooling reds. And, yes, there are so many reds in the area that sometimes the water actually turns bronze. Stories of "acres" of reds roaming the shallows spark much excitement among the Upper Coast angling community. Heck, I'm getting excited just writ-

Upper Laguna Madre is a good place to seize mixed stringers of trout and redfish.

PHOTO BY: GEORGE KNIGHTEN

ing about it, although I believe the term "acre" may be a slight exaggeration of the size of these schools.

The intense fish feeding may last for five minutes or an hour.

We had an odd, on-again, off-again year on Trinity Bay in 2003, but usually things settle into an easy-to-catch pattern come November. These big redfish schools feed on even larger schools of menhaden and shrimp that are making their exodus to the Gulf. The easiest way to find these frenzy feeding schools is by locating diving gulls picking off the nervous baitfish reds push to the surface. However, do not rely solely on birds to find the fish. Anglers typically throw spoons or soft plastic lures for these reds.

During recent autumns, I have used 12-pound-test and a 3/8- to 1/2-ounce jighead to get past the small trout that often hang around the reds. The little specks feed on top and the reds rove around the bottom. Fish down low to get the biggest and best fish.

It is usually better to drift over these schools than to fish them with a trolling motor. In the past, I have approached these big schools by motoring far away from the school to an upcurrent position and then drifting through the feeding action.

UPPER LAGUNA MADRE

Upper Laguna Madre is an underrated destination for redfish. Lots of the time this area turns on in early June when light southeasterly winds push clear water up from Port Mansfield. With the clear waters comes good fishing.

Any of the shorelines of the islands adjacent to the ship channel can provide a good topwater bite early in the mornings, especially when the wind lays. When the tide is low and the sides are dry, work the cuts leading into the Intracoastal. If the tide is in, expect to see tailing reds on the edge of the grass, even during the heat of the day. Stick to spoons, big topwaters, or a Bass Assassin rigged with only a hook for best results.

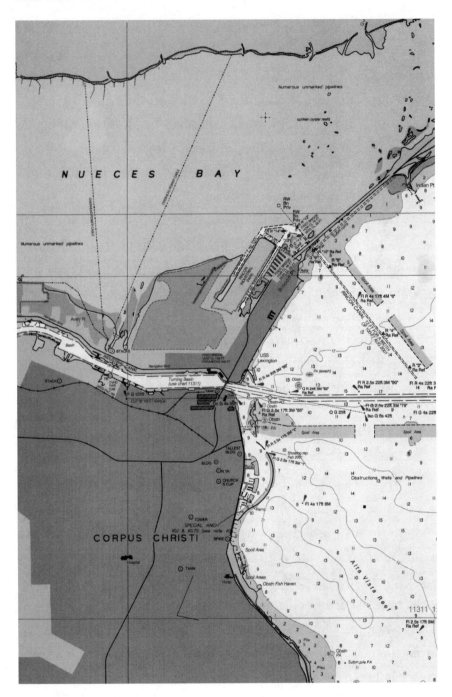

Nueces Bay

Upper Laguna Madre, as it joins Corpus Christi Bay

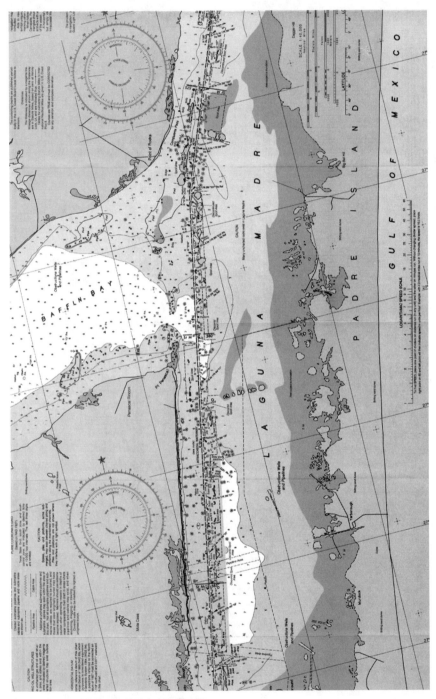

Upper Laguna Madre as it joins Baffin Bay

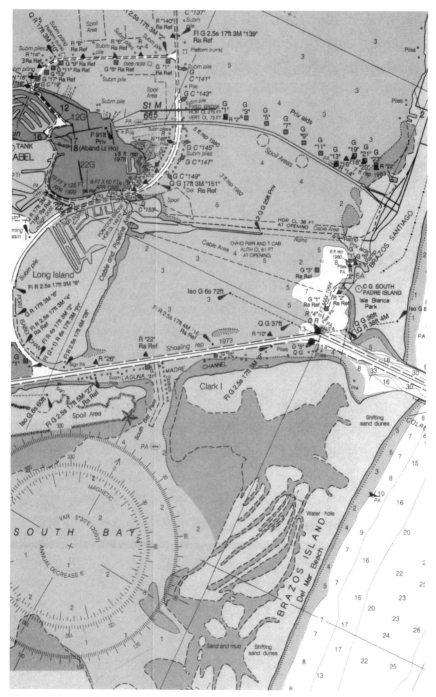

Lower Laguna Madre

Another good method is to drift the shoreline and fish a live shrimp either free-lined or under an Alameda Rattling Float or a Mansfield Mauler rig. This method is especially good when the water is super clear.

Port O'Connor (Gas Wells and Surf)

One of the best places to intercept redfish in Texas is around the gas wells in Espiritu Santo Bay and in the Port O'Connor surf. There are about 20 gas wells in Espiritu. The best way to fish them is to target the shell pads at the bottom. Bouncing a soft plastic will often draw a strike, but fishing with live croaker can be unbelievable. Croaker fishing is very consistent here. Because of their reliability, the gas wells are a good backup plan when you want to go exploring.

Another viable option is running the surf out of Pass Cavalo. When light southeast winds blow, the fishing is tough to beat. Much of this has to do with structure along the beach. The only structure on most beaches is sand and more sand. In this area, there are a number of shrimp boat wrecks that always hold some very large fish in summer. Throwing live croaker around those wrecks is good as is a gold spoon or MirrOlure.

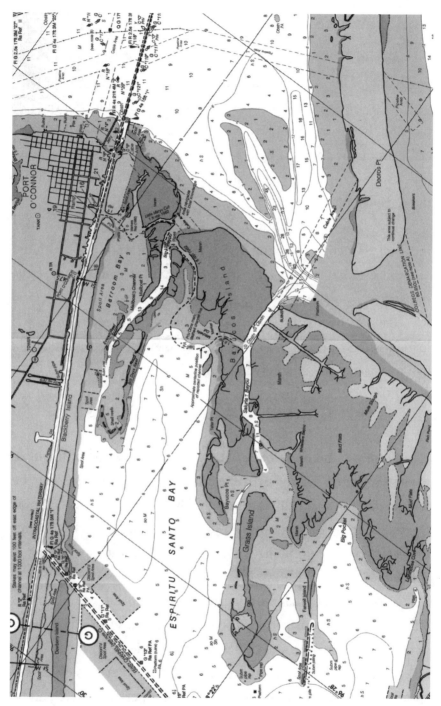

Port O'Connor, and Espiritu Santo Bay.

HANNA'S REEF (GALVESTON BAY)

As noted Upper Coast hotspots go, Hanna's Reef in Galveston Bay is one of the best known. The entire area from the reef to near Lady's Pass and Bull Hill has been a consistent producer of redfish, particularly during the spring and early summer. This area is especially productive when a light wind coincides with a low, incoming tide. These conditions are ideal, but as long as the tide is moving, the reds will bite.

The 51 Series MirrOlures and soft plastics are great to fish over the shell. Someone chucking from a boat might want to go with the 52 Series. Either way, some of the better color patterns are chartreuse, pink, and white with gold sides,

Bass Assassins also work great here. Shell reefs are often loaded with sand eels, which reds love. As such, a soft plastic jerkbait makes a good sand eel imitation.

SOUTH JETTY (PORT ARANSAS)

During summer months, jetties give anglers some of the most consistent action for reds. The South Jetty at Port Aransas may be one of the best (even though it's greatly overlooked) in the Texas Coastal Bend. Pre-dawn runs can yield good fish on black topwater plugs fished right along the rocks, while later in the day the action shifts to live bait.

Croaker is popular with locals, but piggy perch can be just as effective. My best advice would be to fish as close to the rocks as possible since they hold the fish. Look for little holes in the rocks where water can trade from the Gulf to ship channel side. These spots are magnets to reds. Throw your piggy perch in there and be ready.

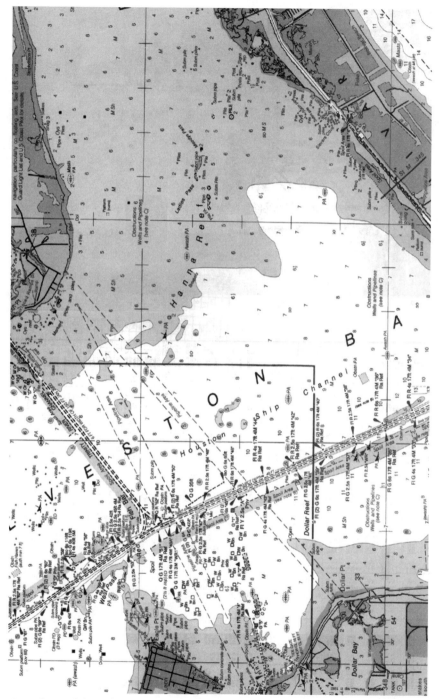

Hannah's Reef (center)

PORT MANSFIELD

Anglers looking to get in on some shallow water wade-fishing have plenty of options at Port Mansfield. Gladys Hole just east of the famous Land Cut is a top wade-fishing destination, although it has a soft bottom. Anglers that are really out of shape might want to pass this one by and let the fitness nuts go at it.

The large sandbar east of Marker 110 gives up its share of redfish, as does Butcher's Island near Marker 113. Butcher's Island the top site to get in on tailing redfish action, and on weekends can be highly pressured. It would be a good idea to get there early during times of heavy boat traffic.

Other good spots include the shorelines near markers 17 and 20 and the East Side of Green Island. This spot can be super for reds, but is very, very shallow and can be treacherous for boaters not used to navigating the area. It is also a good place to get stuck when the tide goes out. If you plan to fish here, pay special attention to the tide tables, else, you could wind up waiting for the tide to come back in.

Port Mansfield is on the shores of Laguna Madre, a shallow body of water along the Intracoastal Canal between the coast and Padre Island. The town is 25 miles from Raymondville on Hwy. 186, which runs into US 77. This is a beautiful stretch of highway to drive, especially for those who like to view wildlife.

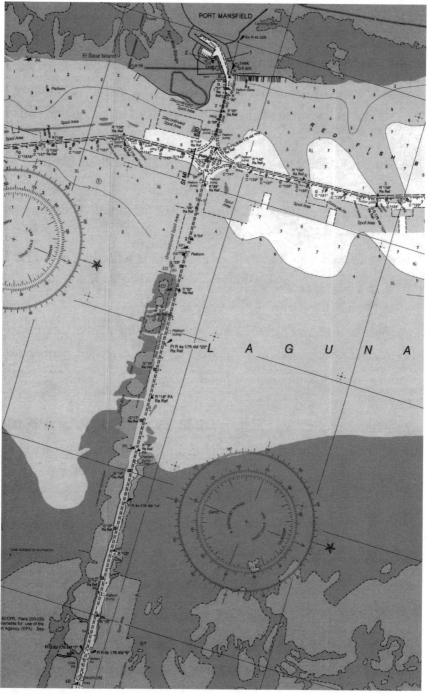

Port Mansfield

Sabine Lake

Sabine redfish start their most consistent bite pattern in summer months, which reaches a dramatic climax in the fall. Summer reds school in the open water of bay systems in mid-day "slick offs." Running the open bay looking for hints of bronze on the water and massive schooling action is the best way to locate these brutes.

In the nearshore Gulf of Mexico out of Sabine pass, big schools of reds chase menhaden and shrimp, most frequently between 200 yards and 2 miles from the beachfront.

Gold spoons and Rat-L-Traps are best for schooling reds in the bays, while the ones offshore turn up their noses to anything except live or fresh-cut fish and crab.

During the early part of fall, the attention turns back to the shorelines. Anglers wading or fishing with carpeted flatbottom boats or skiffs should look for tailing reds or fish cruising along shorelines.

Winter months see redfish action dwindling to near nothing. About the only consistent action is at the Entergy Plant warm water discharge. Bull redfish still haunt the Sabine Jetties.

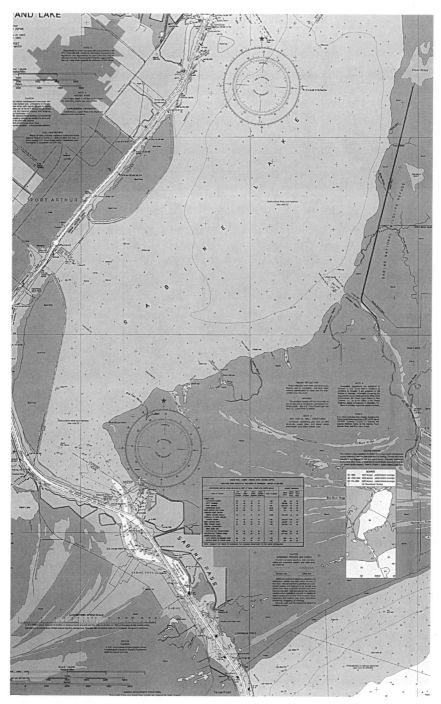

Sabine Lake

KEITH LAKE

Keith Lake is the first of a long series of small lakes that border the town of Sabine Pass, Texas. The area has many sloughs, cuts, and marshy shorelines to fish. One of the best spots is where Keith Lake Cut empties into the lake. There is a spot where sand meets a mud bottom and schools often congregate there.

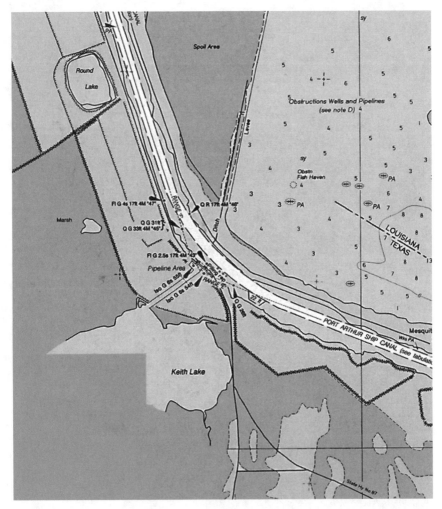

Keith Lake

LAKE CALCASIEU

This Louisiana hotspot is best known for its monster speckled trout, but the redfish action is even better. During spring when the redfish action starts, anglers here have serious problems with the wind. "If the wind blows hard, it's difficult to fish a lot of the open areas, which puts a damper on the trout fishing. That is why a lot of people opt to chase reds in the marsh now," said Ken Chaumont of Bill Lewis Lures, and a landowner on Lake Calcasieu.

"Catching reds on topwaters is lots of fun and has become something people are doing more frequently over here. We've got lots of topwater opportunity and lots of reds to boot," said veteran Big Lake guide and Hackberry Rod & Gun Club owner Capt. Terry Shaughnessy.

Shaughnessy said that during the later summer to early fall period, the shoreline along the Cameron Prairie Refuge is one of the best spots for reds in this ecosystem: "During fall, the shoreline over there can be just alive with fish. Reds and specks are actively feeding and are easy to locate, even for anglers who might not be familiar with the area. The key is to not allow all of the action to confuse you, and stick with a proven producing pattern. This usually pays off."

What he means by "sticking with proven producers" is to go with patterns that have proved successful year in and year out. If you want to catch fish on topwaters, then stay with them. If you are looking for numbers go with plastics.

Anglers with carpeted flatbottom boats or skiffs should look for tailing reds or fish cruising along shorelines. A way to increase the odds of seeing these fish is to wear polarized sunglasses, which takes the glare off the water and allows you to see into the water much better.

Capt. Erik Rue said there are plenty other great spots for red in Lake Calcasieu: "There are lots of great places during later summer and early fall. Turney's Bay gets good going into fall and can be good in summer as well, although the pattern is live bait. The good thing about summer is the lack of wind, which helps the water clarity in that area. We have such a muddy bottom in a very shallow lake that it does not take much of a wind to stir it up. Turney's Bay is best on a light wind out of the north or the west with an outgoing tide."

Commissary Point is one of the areas I fished with Chaumont a couple of years ago. It is in the middle of the lake along the eastern shoreline just south of Hebert's Landing. Rue said of it: "Commissary Point is a good spot to hit after most of the boats have left and the water clears. The key here is bait. It's deeper than much of the lake and always has a steady bait supply and good numbers of fish."

Rue said anglers looking for big fish should hit Lambert's Bayou, Lambert's Bayou Reef, or Grand Bayou: "Those are good spots to catch big fish on live bait, or to throw topwaters. Lots of huge fish have been caught there in recent years."

One of my Dad's favorite spots from yesteryear that still produces today is the old rock jetties along the southern shoreline of the lake. The rocks there hold lots of baitfishes, shrimp, and plenty of hefty reds. Rue prefers to fish the jetties on a light incoming tide, and looks for concentrations of mullet to find fish. The Old Jetties are also a great spot for anglers to fish at night. Green lights set up along the rocks can draw in incredible concentrations of baitfish, and therefore equally impressive numbers of reds. Live shrimp is a good choice for night fishing, but soft plastics in glow, chartreuse, or white colors also yield strong catches.

CONSTANCE BEACH

Located just south of Lake Calcasieu, Constance Beach offers some of the best surf fishing for reds in Louisiana. Many big bulls run this beach beginning in the summer, with peak action around the middle of October. What makes Constance Beach so great is the system of rock jetties. The rocks hold many crab, and in turn lots of redfish. Anglers wanting to catch the Big One should fish with crab, cut mullet, or croaker out past the rocks. For anglers wanting to tangle with big reds on lighter gear, chunk D.O.A. Shrimp or gold spoons along the rocks. This, by the way, is Capt. Terry Shaughnessy's favorite spot to catch bull redfish.

CHANDELEUR ISLANDS

These barrier islands located off the coasts of Louisiana and Mississippi are known widely for their phenomenal speckled trout fishing, but they are loaded with redfish. Any of the islands can hold reds, but the shallow coves of Breton Island and the surf side of the big islands near Biloxi holds lots of them. Give the nearby oil rigs a try. They are loaded with big bulls.

COCODRIE, LOUISIANA

The marshes of Cocodrie in southern Louisiana are some of the most fertile in the world and, boy, do they produce reds. Fly-fishermen flock to the area to seek tailing reds in the shallow flats and cuts.

BANK-FISHING HOTSPOTS

Having to fish from the bank is not an enviable task. Most of the best fishing spots are not accessible to bank-fishermen, and those that can be reached from land are often crowded. Nonetheless, land-bound anglers in Texas have it better than folks in other areas. We have plentiful access to good bank-fishing, especially in saltwater. Some areas are well known and can be highly pressured at times, while others see little pressure. The following are some of the best bank-fishing spots on the coast.

PLEASURE ISLAND

Located on the west bank of Lake Sabine, Pleasure Island offers miles of access to bank-fishing. One of the best spots is at the causeway bridge at the Texas/Louisiana border on Highway 82. The area around the bridge is excellent during spring and fall. Less than 100 yards from the bridge is the Walter Umphrey Pier, a free, lighted fishing pier.

The other popular fishing areas here are the north and south revetment walls. A public road runs alongside the walls. Anglers can fish either from the rocks or from one of several small, free fishing piers that dot the wall. Anglers can also fish and crab in the revetment ponds themselves. They are great spots to catch redfish.

To get to Pleasure Island take the Highway 73 in Port Arthur to the Highway 82 (Martin Luther King) Exit. Follow 82 over the Martin Luther King Bridge and you are on Pleasure Island.

TEXAS BAYOU

Texas Bayou, located in Sabine Pass, feeds into the Sabine-Neches ship channel about one mile north of the jetties. A bridge and dock provide good fishing for reds. Crabbing is also good here.

To get to Texas Bayou take Highway 87 to Sabine Pass. When

Pleasure Island

you get there, go straight at the four-way and follow the curving road to the left. About 1/4 mile down the road, you will see a stop sign. From there take a right and follow the road for a mile until you reach a small bridge. That's Texas Bayou.

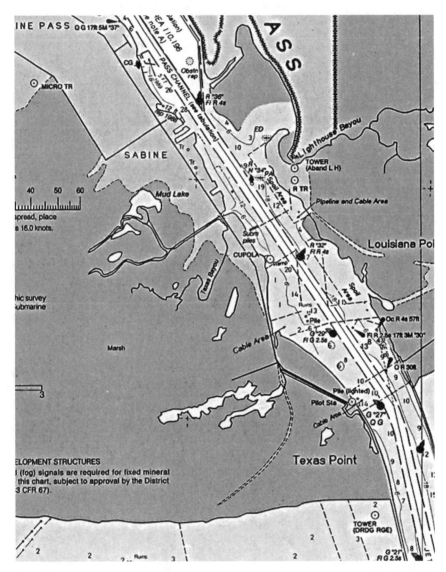

Texas Bayou

DICK DOWLING PARK

Years ago, Dick Dowling Park used to be a popular redfish spot. Fewer anglers fish there now, but the fishing can still be good. If you decided to fish here, bring a rod that can cast a long way.

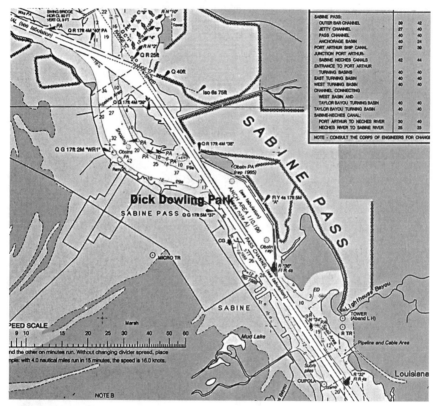

Dick Dowling Park

There are many hang-ups just off the bank.

To get to Dick Dowling Park, take Highway 87 to Sabine Pass. When you get there, go straight at the four-way and follow the curving road to the left. You will see the park signs on the left side.

Twin Lakes

Twin Lakes just outside of Bridge City has been popular with bank-fishermen for years. The fishing is good because of the diversity of habitat. There is a deep canal on one side and shallow marsh on the other. This is where I cut my teeth fishing by catching redfish, black drum, flounder, and garfish.

Some of the best spots include the deeper water around the bridge and along the saltwater barrier. Most of the fishing is on the side of the road where the power plant is located. The lake on the opposite side of the road is fishable, but it is extremely shallow. There are two culverts here, which allow water to exchange from both sides of the highway. These are good spots to crab and catch live bait.

The Twin Lakes are located between Bridge City and Port Arthur on Highway 87

Lake Road

More commonly known as "Bailey Road" because the Bailey family has operated a bait camp there for years, the Lake Road area offers good fishing. The area near Bailey's Bait Camp allows access to wade-fish Sabine Lake in Old River Cover, which is one of my old standbys for reds.

Lake Road is located at the last red light leaving Bridge City toward Port Arthur on Highway 87. That would be the first red light coming from Port Arthur.

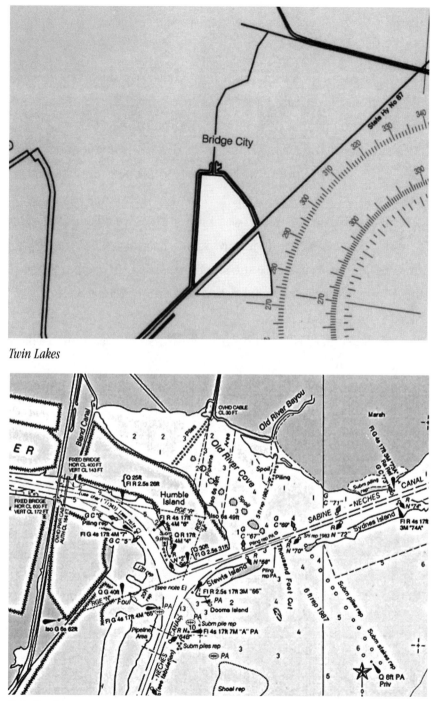

Twin Lakes

Lake Road

Rollover Pass

Created in 1954 as a link to East Galveston Bay from the Gulf of Mexico, Rollover Pass has consistently ranked as one of the most popular bank-fishing destinations on the Upper Coast. That is because anglers can fish along both sides of the pass and waders have easy access to prime wading on the flats near the channel on the north end.

The best bait for reds is something live. Live shrimp fall easily to bait stealers, so mud minnows, shad, and croaker are better choices. Mud minnows are the standard issue in these parts due to the excellent flounder fishing, and will more than suffice for the other popular game fish.

Rollover Pass is located on Highway 87 between High Island and Galveston.

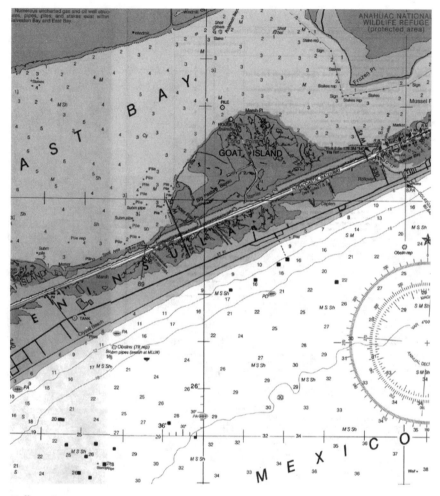

Rollover Pass

COPANO CAUSEWAY PIER (ARANSAS BAY)

Located on Highway 35 N, the pier divides Copano Bay and Aransas Bay. It is lighted, has cleaning tables, and is open seven days a week, 24 hours a day. Contact the north end at 361-729-8519, the south end at 361-729-7762.

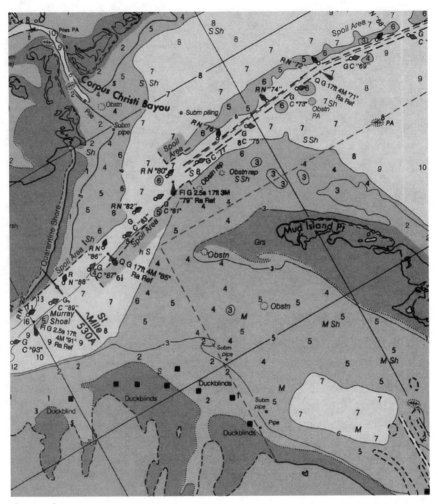

Copano Causeway

ARANSAS NATIONAL WILDLIFE REFUGE

Located along San Antonio and Aransas Bays, the 70,504 acres of the Aransas National Wildlife Refuge is well known for its resident wildlife and winter whooping cranes. There are some fine fishing opportunities to be found there, too. For more information, call 512-286-3559.

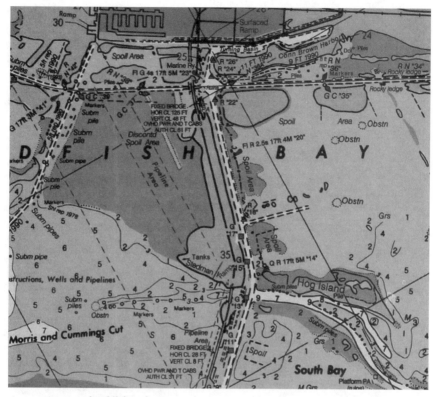

Aransas National Wildlife Refuge

HUMBLE CHANNEL AT THE JFK CAUSEWAY (CORPUS CHRISTI)

Located between Baffin Bay and Port Aransas, this area is a favorite of experienced bank-fishermen. There are two piers, one at Trainer's Marina, another at Red Dot Bait Stand. This is an excellent place to catch redfish, particularly during the fall months.

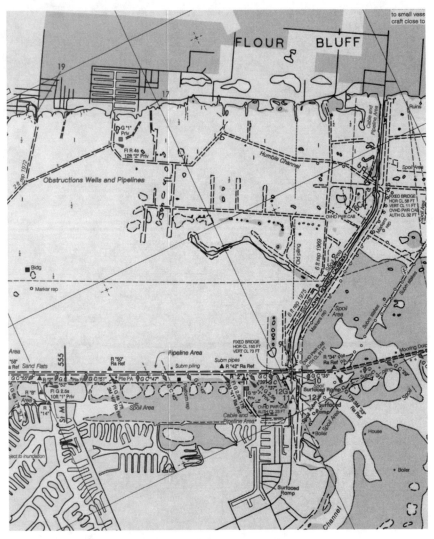

Humble Channel @ JFK Causeway (Corpus)

Goose Island State Park

This 321-acre park is surrounded by Aransas and St. Charles Bays and offers anglers a good chance at redfish. The shoreline is comprised of concrete bulkhead, oyster shell, mud, flat and marsh grass. Anglers fishing along the concrete bulkhead with cane poles and live shrimp occasionally pull up big reds. Most anglers fish with

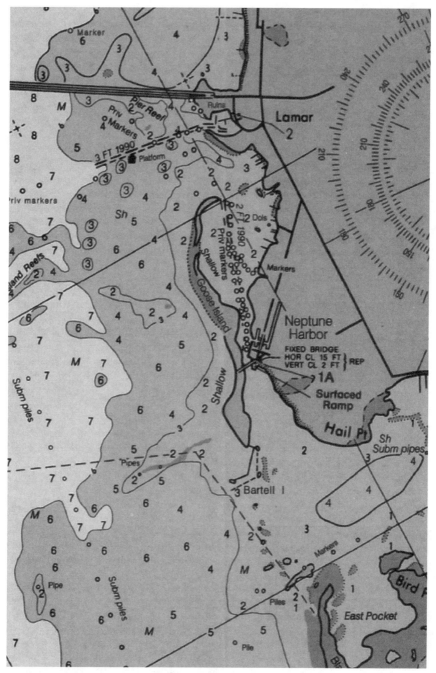

Goose Island

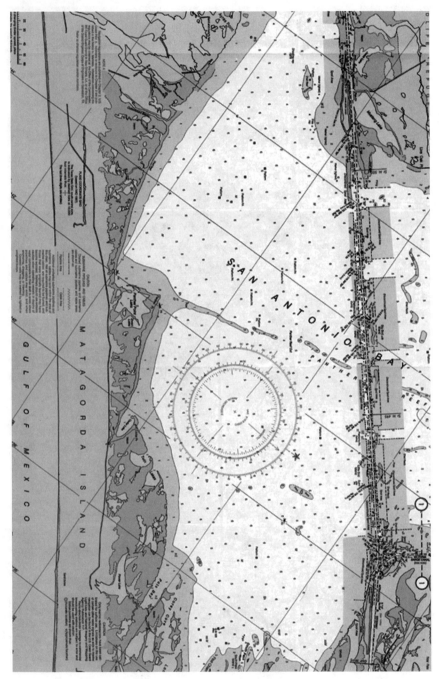

Matagorda Island State Park (Port O'Connor)

crab or mullet out in the bay. Facilities include a fish cleaning shelter and a 1,620-foot lighted pier with two fish-cleaning tables. For more information, call 361-729-2858.

MATAGORDA ISLAND STATE PARK (PORT O'CONNOR)

If seclusion is your idea of a good time, then this is your spot. This is one of the best spots in the state to catch bull redfish in the late summer and fall.

The surf gets deep quick, so be careful when wading out to cast a surf rod, and be especially careful at night—when the big sharks will be prowling. More than likely, they will not attack you, but if you smell like menhaden or bloody mullet, there is no telling what might happen. Use your head because Matagorda Island is a long way from a hospital. For more information, call 361-983-2215.

OCEAN DRIVE (CORPUS CHRISTI)

This drive will take you along the main shoreline of Corpus Christi Bay near Cole Park Pier, Oso Pier, and other bank- and wade-fishing locations.

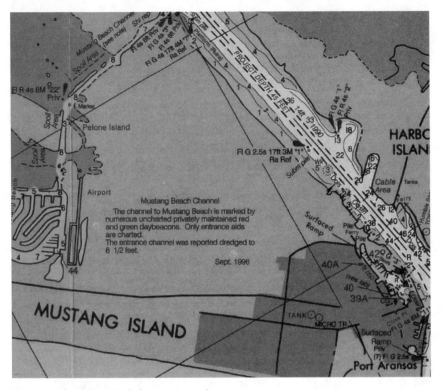

Mustang Island State Park (Port O'Connor)

MUSTANG ISLAND STATE PARK (PORT ARANSAS)

This 3,954-acre park offers five miles of beach on the Gulf of Mexico, and it is loaded with redfish. This is a secluded, unique ecosystem dependent upon sand dunes. Coastal dunes are the product of wind-deposited sand anchored by sparse mats of vegetation. The height of well-vegetated dunes may reach 35 feet in some areas of the park. If you plan on doing much walking, be prepared to contend with the dunes. If you plan on driving down the beach, be careful not to get stuck. The sand here is infamous for that. For more information, call 512-389-8900.

CAMERON COUNTY PARKS (HARLINGEN)

The Cameron County Park System leases property from the Laguna Atascosa National Wildlife Refuge along the Arroyo Colorado River. Adolph Thomae, Jr., County Park provides fishing piers and a boat launch along with RV and campsites. The fishing here ranges from fair to good for redfish. For more information, call 956-748-2044.

PADRE ISLAND NATIONAL SEASHORE

This is Texas' single largest bank-fishing spot. Counting both sides of the island, there are more than 150 miles of fishing holes covering the Gulf of Mexico and Laguna Madre. It offers the bulk of South Texas bank-fishing.

According to U.S. Fish and Wildlife Service officials, Padre Island National Seashore encompasses 133,000 acres of America's vanishing barrier islands. It is the longest remaining undeveloped barrier island in the world. Part of Padre Island's greatness as a fishing destination comes from its diversity. Waders can venture chest-deep into the blue-green waters and chuck surface lures for slot-sized reds, while their counterparts battle big bull sharks on surf rods from the white sand beaches.

The biggest problem with Padre Island is its remoteness. There is a whole lot of island that sees very few people due to the inhospitable nature of the sand dunes. Some of the easier places to reach are Malaquite Beach, a semi-primitive campground with water, restrooms, showers and a concession stand with plenty of excellent fishing holes. There is also Bird Island Basin, which offers great fishing and a very primitive campsite with only pit toilets.

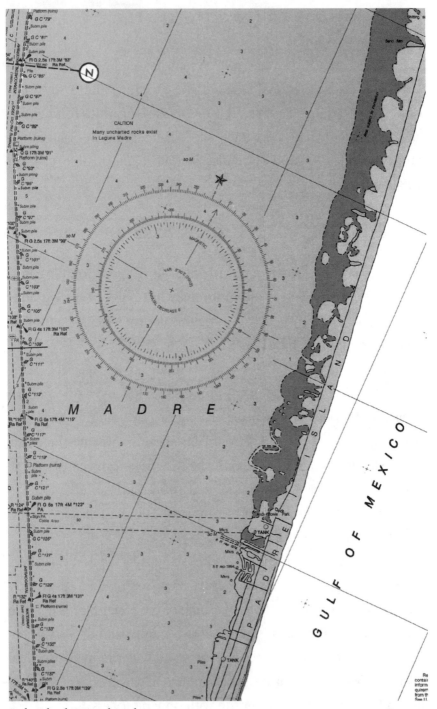

Padre Island National Seashore

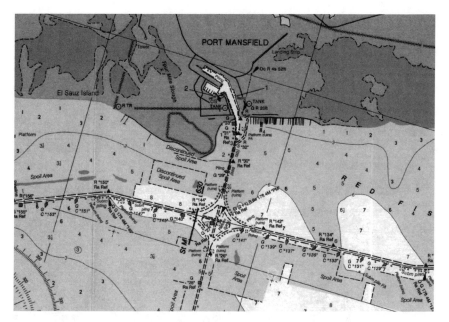

Willacy County Park Pier (Port Mansfield)

WILLACY COUNTY PARK PIER (PORT MANSFIELD)

This 500-foot lighted pier offers good access to Laguna Madre and routinely produces good catches of reds in the summer and spring months. Besides the pier, there are also picnic tables, barbecue pits, and restrooms. For more information, call 956-944-4000.

BOCA CHICA STATE PARK (PORT ISABEL)

Boca Chica State Park is just under 1,100 acres, located in the Boca Chica Subdelta of the Rio Grande River, in southeastern Cameron County. The south shore of South Bay, west shore of Boca Chica Bay, and the flat, sandy, northern end of Boca Chica Island are prime redfish spots. The water is generally very clear, so adjust fishing tactics accordingly and look for drop-offs from the shallow water. Most of the aquatic terrain here is flat, and even the slightest depth change will hold fish. For more information, call 956-585-1107.

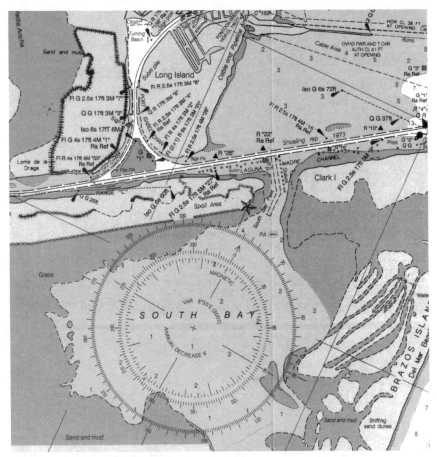

Boca Chica State Park (Port Isabel)

Chapter Nine

Redfish Recipes

Redfish are tops in the frying pan, on the grill or in the oven. Their flesh has a mild taste and texture, and they yield a lot of meat per pound of fish. The following recipes are some I have tried over the years, some from anglers in Texas, Louisiana, and Florida. They range from simple to quite elaborate.

Enjoy.

REDFISH ON THE HALF SHELL

1 fresh redfish

onion powder, garlic powder, salt, pepper

1 12-oz beer, strong

1/4 stick butter

1 Tbs. Worcestershire

1 clove garlic, crushed

1 tsp Caribbean jerk seasoning

Fillet the fish leaving the skin and scales on. Lay the fillet skin side down. Sprinkle flesh side with onion power, fresh garlic, salt, and pepper, and rub in with your fingers. Put the fish in the fridge for one to two hours to marinate. Make the following sauce just before taking the fish out of the fridge.

In a medium saucepan, combine beer, butter, Worcestershire sauce, garlic, jerk seasoning, and a little pepper. Stir ingredients over a medium flame until blended and butter is melted. Oil the skin side of the redfish and then place the fish skin side down on a hot grill. Baste the flesh with the sauce every 10 minutes. Cook the fish 30 to 45 minutes over low to medium heat. The skin will curl up, keeping the sauce on the meat and making it very moist. Fish flakes easily when done. Remove fish from the grill; most of the scales will stay on the grill.

BLACKENED REDFISH

6 8- to 10-oz. fish fillets, 1/2 to 3/4 inches thick

1/2 lb. unsalted butter, melted

1/2 Tbs. paprika

2 1/2 tsp. salt

1 tsp. onion powder

1 tsp. garlic powder

1 tsp. ground red pepper

3/4 tsp. white pepper

1/2 tsp. black pepper

1/2 tsp. dried thyme

1/2 tsp. dried oregano

Combine seasonings. (A prepared blackened seasoning may be substituted.) Cook outdoors as it creates copious smoke.

Heat a large cast iron skillet over high heat. Dip each fillet in butter and coat with seasoning mix. Place in hot skillet and top with one tsp. butter. Cook uncovered over high heat about two minutes. Turn and cook two more minutes, serve immediately.

Royal Redfish

4 redfish, skinned and filleted (5 pounds)

1/2 cup oil

1/2 cup flour

2 med. onions, chopped

1 clove garlic, minced

1/2 cup celery, chopped

1/2 cup green pepper, chopped

1 8-oz. can tomato sauce

1 14-1/2-oz. can tomatoes

1/4 cup parsley, chopped

1 bay leaf

1/2 tsp. allspice

pinch of basil

2 sprigs saffron

1 cup water

1 cup red wine (Burgundy)

salt and pepper, to taste

lemon juice

Make a medium-dark roux with oil and flour in a large skillet (cast iron is best). Add onion, green pepper, celery, and garlic to roux and sauté until tender. Add tomato sauce, tomatoes, parsley, rest of seasonings, salt, and pepper to taste. Simmer slowly for 35 minutes. (At this point, you may freeze for later use.) Add water slowly and cook down to thick gravy. Add wine and more water (if needed) to make sauce medium thick. Rub fish with lemon, salt and pepper lightly, and then place in large baking dish. Pour sauce over fish and bake 40 to 50 minutes or until flaky in preheated 350 oven.

Redfish Beignets

3 pounds redfish

hot sauce

3 cups flour

1 cup cornstarch

1 Tbs. paprika

1 tsp. cayenne pepper

2 Tbs. salt

1/2 tsp. garlic powder

Marinate redfish in hot sauce for 1 hour or more. Combine remaining ingredients to make breading. Roll redfish in breading and deep fry at 350 until fish pieces float. Remove from deep fry and place on a paper towel.

Make a sauce by combining:

1 cup mayonnaise

1/4 cup sour cream

1 Tbs. Dijon mustard

salt and pepper to taste

Place a lettuce leaf on a salad plate. Spoon beignet sauce onto lettuce. Place redfish beignets on plate. Garnish with a carrot curl and chopped parsley, and serve.

Sausage Crusted Redfish with Shoestring Potatoes

6 Tbs. olive oil

2 zucchini, sliced lengthwise into 1-inch thick slices

2 yellow squash, sliced lengthwise into 1-inch thick slices

2 eggplant, sliced lengthwise into 1-inch thick slices

1 cup roasted pecan pieces

2 tsp. garlic, chopped

1/4 cup green onions, chopped

3/4 cup Worcestershire sauce

2 med lemons, skin and pith removed

2 bay leaves

3/4 cup cold butter, cubed

3 oz. smoked sausage, finely diced

1 cup breadcrumbs

1 Tbs. Cajun seasoning

4 6- to 8-oz. redfish fillets

2 cups shoestring potatoes

chives

Parmesan cheese

salt and pepper to taste

Preheat oven to 450. Season the vegetables with two Tbs. olive oil, salt, and pepper. Place in a roasting pan and roast for 10 minutes. Remove from oven and cool. Dice and set aside.

In a large sauté pan, cook roasted vegetables, pecans, and garlic in 1 Tbs. Olive oil for two minutes, season with salt and pepper. Stir in green onions and keep warm. In a saucepan, combine the Worcestershire sauce, lemons, and bay leaves. Simmer until reduced by 2/3. Whisk in butter cubes one at a time. The sauce should be thick and coat the back of a spoon. Keep warm. In a hot sauté pan, steam the sausage for two minutes with a few Tbs. of water. Remove from heat and cool completely. Turn sausage into a mixing bowl and combine with breadcrumbs.

Season fillets with Cajun seasoning. In a large, ovenproof sauté pan, heat the remaining olive oil. Add redfish, topside down. Sauté four minutes and turn. Cover the top of each fillet with a quarter of the sausage crust. Place sauté pan in oven and cook for minutes.

To assemble, spoon the sauce in the center and around the rim of each plate. Mound the shoestrings in the center of each plate, then place fillet to the side. Garnish with red and yellow peppers, chives, and cheese.

CREOLE REDFISH

6 lbs. redfish fillets

1/4 lb. butter

6 onions, chopped

1 bell pepper

4 sticks celery, chopped

1 cup shallots, chopped

3 whole pickles (any kind)

25 pimento stuffed olives

1/2 cup fresh parsley, chopped

4 cloves garlic, minced

1 cup fresh sliced mushrooms

3 tsp. Worcestershire

1 lemon sliced

juice of two lemons

Melt butter in a large cast iron pot. Sauté onions until brown. Add bell pepper, celery, and shallots, cook until tender. Add remaining ingredients except fish, lemon juice, and lemon slices. Cook 20 minutes. Place redfish in roasting pan and cover with sauce. Sprinkle with lemon juice and garnish with lemon slices. Bake in 350 oven 1-1/2 to 2 hours.

BARBECUED REDFISH

1 5- to 6-lb. redfish, whole cleaned

1 bell pepper, chopped

3 sticks celery, chopped

3 cloves garlic, chopped

1 medium onion, chopped

2 8-oz. bottles Zesty Italian salad dressing

1 cup white wine

2 Tbs. Worcestershire

2 sticks butter or margarine

1/2 can beer

2 Tbs. catsup

salt and pepper to taste

Cook all ingredients except fish about 90 minutes on a low fire in a 2-quart saucepan. Stir occasionally to keep from sticking. Place fish in roasting pan and fill inside with ingredients. Cook on barbecue pit uncovered for 45 minutes to one hour, basting every 15 to 20 minutes. Salt and pepper to taste.

REDFISH CASSEROLE

2 lb. redfish fillets

1/2 cup Creamy Italian salad dressing

1/2 cup butter, melted

1-1/2 cups Potato chips, crumbled

8 slices American cheese

(Note: Do not use ridged potato chips and use only "creamy" dressing.)

Place fish in a 9x12 baking dish. Pour salad dressing and melted butter over fish. Sprinkle with potato chips and add cheese slices. Bake 15 minutes in a preheated 350 oven.

REDFISH WITH BASIL BUTTER

4 6-oz. redfish fillets

1/4 tsp. Paprika

1/2 cup slivered fresh basil

2 Tbs. unsalted butter

2 Tbs. olive oil

2 Tbs. fresh lemon juice

salt and pepper to taste

Preheat broiler. Cover a baking sheet with foil. Melt butter in small saucepan, add olive oil and lemon juice, cook 5 minutes over low heat. Cover and remove pan from heat. Lay fillets on baking sheet and season with a bit of the butter sauce, salt, pepper, and paprika. Broil 4 minutes as close to heat source as possible. Transfer to serving plates and top with remaining lemon butter sauce, sprinkle with fresh basil.

BROILED CHEESY REDFISH

2 lbs. redfish fillets

2 Tbs. lemon juice

1/2 cup Parmesan cheese

1/4 cup butter, softened

3 Tbs. mayonnaise

3 green onions, chopped

1/4 tsp. salt

dash of hot sauce

Place fillets in a single layer on a greased, shallow oven-to-table type broiler pan. Brush with lemon juice. Combine remaining ingredients in a small bowl and set aside. Broil fillets until fish flakes easily when tested with a fork. Remove from oven and spread with cheese mixture. Broil an additional 30 seconds or until cheese is lightly browned and bubbly. Garnish with lemon twists and parsley if desired

CRISPY PECAN REDFISH

1-1/2 lbs. redfish fillets

1 cup milk

2 cup yellow cornmeal

1 tsp. hot sauce

1/2 tsp. salt

1 stick unsalted butter

1/4 cup vegetable oil

1 cup chopped pecans

1 cup chopped parsley

1/2 cup freshly squeezed lemon juice

Wash fillets under cold running water and place in a bowl with milk, hot sauce, and salt. Allow to sit 15 minutes at room temperature. Heat 2 Tbs. butter and vegetable oil in a skillet over medium high heat. Drain fillets and dredge in cornmeal. Fry until crispy and brown, about two minutes on a side; do not crowd the pan. Pour grease out of skillet and add remaining butter. Place over medium heat, add nuts when butter melts. Stir constantly while the nuts brown. Add parsley and lemon juice, stir to combine. Pour sauce over fillets and serve immediately.

PACKET REDFISH

1 lb redfish fillets

2 Tbs. margarine or butter

1/4 cup lemon juice

1 Tbs. chopped parsley

1 tsp. dill weed

1 tsp. salt

1/4 tsp. pepper

1 med. onion, thinly sliced

Paprika

On four large buttered squares of heavy-duty aluminum foil, place equal amounts of fish. In small saucepan, melt margarine, add lemon juice, parsley, dill weed, salt, and pepper. Pour equal amounts over fish. Sprinkle with paprika, top with onion slices. Wrap foil securely around fish, leaving space for fish to expand. Grill or broil 5 to 7 minutes on each side or until fish flakes with fork.

PICKLED REDFISH

2 lbs. redfish fillets

1/2 cup vinegar

4 oz green chili peppers

1 Tbs. orange peel, finely shredded

1/4 cup orange juice

1/4 cup onion, chopped

2 bay leaves

2 cloves garlic, minced

1 orange; thinly sliced

Rinse, seed, and chop green chilies. Place fish fillets in 10-inch skillet, cover with boiling water, simmer covered, 5 to 8 minutes or until fish flakes easily when tested with a fork. Drain, arrange in a shallow dish. Combine vinegar, oil, chili peppers, orange peel, orange juice, onion, bay leaves, garlic, 1 tsp salt, and 1/8 tsp. pepper. Pour over fish. Cover and refrigerate several hours or overnight. Drain off marinade and transfer fish to a serving dish. Serve cold, garnished with orange slices.

REDFISH TACOS

12 Redfish fillets (1-1/2 oz. ea.)

12 corn tortillas

1 cup flour

1 cup beer

garlic powder

pepper

cabbage leaves, chopped medium

1/2 cup mayonnaise

1/2 cup yogurt

salsa

lime wedges

Combine mayonnaise and yogurt, set aside. Mix flour, garlic powder, and pepper. Stir beer into flour mixture until well blended. Wash fish by dipping in cold, lightly salted water. Dry thoroughly and dip in flour batter. Deep fry at 375 until golden brown and crispy.

Heat corn tortillas until soft and hot. On each tortilla, layer fish fillet, mayonnaise mixture, salsa, and cabbage. Top off with squeeze of lime. Fold tortilla over to serve.

SALSA

1 garlic clove, minced

6 tomatoes, peeled, seeded, and diced

1/2 onion, minced

2 Tbs. cilantro leaves, chopped, stems removed

2 jalapeno chilies, seeded and chopped

1-1/2 tsp. salt

1/4 tsp. pepper

Combine ingredients and mix well.

Redfish Special

1 lb. redfish fillets
3/4 tsp. seasoned salt
juice of 1 lemon
1/2 pint sour cream
1/4 lb. cheddar cheese

Sprinkle fillets with seasoned salt and lemon juice. Place in broiler pan and broil until fish flakes. Spread with sour cream and sprinkle with grated cheese. Return to oven and broil until cheese melts and cream is bubbly.

Redfish Margarita

4 redfish filets
flour
1/4 cup peanut oil
3 Tbs. butter
1-1/2 oz. tequila
1/2 oz. triple sec
1 Tbs. lime juice
2 Tbs. minced parsley
salt and pepper

Dredge fish in flour and shake off excess. Heat oil in skillet over moderate heat and cook fish 3 to 4 minutes per side or until just done. Remove and keep warm. Discard oil and add butter to pan. When melted, carefully add tequila (it may flame). Add remaining ingredients and cook until the butter foams. Pour over fish and serve.

REDFISH CROQUETTES

2 Tbs. margarine
3 Tbs. cornstarch
3/4 tsp. salt
1/4 tsp. pepper
1 cup milk
3 cups cooked, flaked redfish
1-1/2 Tbs. chopped parsley
1 tsp. lemon juice
1/2 tsp. grated onion

Melt margarine in sauce pan. Blend in cornstarch, salt, and pepper. Remove from heat. Gradually add milk, mixing until smooth. Cook over medium heat, stirring constantly, until mixture thickens and comes to a boil. Boil 1 minute. Stir in remaining ingredients, chill. Shape, roll in dry breadcrumbs, then in slightly beaten egg, then in crumbs again. Pan or deep fry in corn oil until golden brown.

REDFISH PONCHATRAIN

4 8-oz. redfish fillets

1 cup white crabmeat

1/2 lb. small to medium shrimp, peeled

12 to 14 fresh oysters

6 Tbs. unsalted butter

2 cups seasoned flour

2 Tbs. fresh lemon juice

In a large skillet, melt 4 Tbs. butter over medium-high heat. Dredge fillets in seasoned flour, sauté until golden brown. Remove from skillet to warm platter. Reserve pan juices. Add two table-spoons butter to pan juices, sauté shrimp, crabmeat, and oysters until shrimp turns pink. Add lemon juice, shake pan gently. Top fillets with seafood and serve.

SWEET ONION CRUSTED REDFISH

1 lb. Onion, slivered and fried until crisp

2 cups breadcrumbs

1 Tbs. garlic powder

1 Tbs. onion powder

1 Tbs. minced basil

1 Tbs. minced parsley

1 tsp. salt

1 cup seasoned flour

Toss breadcrumbs, onion, herbs, and spices together in steel bowl. Dredge redfish seasoned flour. Egg wash crust with bread-crumb mixture. Sauté in a large pan over medium heat until done.

SWEET AND SOUR REDFISH

2 lbs. redfish fillets

1 cup flour

1/2 cup cornstarch

2 tsp. baking powder

1 tsp. baking soda

1-1/2 cups cold water (very important that the water is cold, as the batter is very thin)

1 tsp. salt

sweet and sour sauce

Mix batter ingredients and dip dry fish fillets into batter. Let excess drip back into batter bowl. Drop fillets into deep fryer and cook until fish floats or is golden brown. Serve with sweet and sour sauce

SWEET AND SOUR SAUCE

1-1/2 cup pineapple juice

1 cup sugar

3 Tbs. cornstarch

6 Tbs. vinegar

6 Tbs. catsup

Combine sugar and cornstarch. Blend in vinegar and catsup. Stir in pineapple juice. Cook, stirring, until thickened and clear. Keep sauce warm until needed.

Chapter Ten

Future of the Redfish

To look at where the future of redfish is heading, it is necessary to first take a brief look at the past. For many years, commercial fishermen targeted redfish heavily with gill nets, purse seines, and other highly effective tools. Fisheries agencies even allowed recreational anglers to use gill nets in Texas to catch reds and other popular fishes. My dad used to run a gill net when he was a kid and talked about catching entire schools of fish at a time. Now it seems like a waste, but back then that was the way people did things.

By the 1970's, the American public fell in love with redfish, partly because of New Orleans Chef Paul Prudhomme's famous "blackened redfish" recipe. The result was that redfish populations were ravaged, and recreational fishermen experienced terrible fishing conditions. A group of concerned coastal anglers fought to get the redfish classified as a game fish and therefore protected from commercial harvest. Many outdoor writers call those days the "redfish wars," which spawned the Gulf Coast Conservation Association (GCCA), now Coastal Conservation Association (CCA).

The banning of commercial redfish harvest along with aggres-

Capt. Robert Vail hands over a pair of live redfish to the Texas Parks & Wildlife Department to help strengthen their stocking program.

sive stocking efforts spearheaded by GCCA and the Texas Parks & Wildlife Department (TPWD) gave the redfish population a much-needed boost. At the time of this writing, Texas has stocked more than 100,000,000 redfish fingerlings into coastal bay systems and estuaries. TPWD officials also placed a slot limit on redfish that protected the mature breeding specimens (bull reds) from harvest.

By the early 1990's, redfish numbers had stabilized and recreational fishermen started catching lots of them. In fact, by 1994 red-fish numbers got so high that TPWD biologists decided it was okay for anglers to harvest a couple of bull redfish each year. TPWD initiated a special red drum "trophy tag."

Fast forward to the New Millennium. Now, redfish are a "pestilence." Since given protection from commercial harvest, their numbers have skyrocketed to the point of overpopulation. Much like snow geese, which are on the verge of permanently destroying their own arctic nesting grounds, redfish are causing ecological damage in Texas bay systems. Specifically, they, along with record numbers of speckled trout, are responsible for declines in shrimp populations. Redfish are also responsible for causing severe declines in the number and average size of blue crabs in the marshes of Louisiana. There are simply too may crustacean-loving reds prowling the estuarine waters of the Sportsman's Paradise.

If you think that sounds far-fetched, you are right.

Absurd or not, such ideas were recently pitched as legitimate concerns to TPWD and the Louisiana Department of Wildlife & Fisheries (LDWF) by representatives of the commercial fishing industry. When state regulators decided to lessen the scope of the commercial shrimp and crab fleet, those industries decided to turn on the sport fish species popular with recreational anglers and in particular target the redfish as a scapegoat.

"It's hard to believe they would actually blame sport fish stocks for the decline of shrimp in Texas, but they did," said TPWD Coastal Fisheries Director Hal Osburn. "I'm sure not all of the shrimpers felt this way, but there was certainly an extreme contingent that tried to sell it to us."

An official with LDWF who requested anonymity pointed out

that commercial crabbers have brought the redfish up on several occasions and have managed to get the attention of high-ranking legislators: "You would think such statements would be laughed off, but there are actually a few legislators taking this stuff seriously. Actually, the word is that some of them are just looking for any excuse to make the redfish a commercial species. There's a strong movement among some of the commercial guys to make this happen, and I would certainly advise recreational anglers interested in the future of this currently magnificent fishery to be on guard. There seems to be something in the cards for commercializing redfish."

That "something" may already be taking place. In 2001, the Red Drum Advisory Panel (RDAP) of the Gulf of Mexico Fisheries Management Council (GMFMC) asked federal fisheries managers to consider a "limited commercial season" for redfish. They passed on it the first time, but sources say the concept is gaining serious momentum again.

Before venturing farther into this sea of bureaucracy, let's examine the roles of these agencies.

The GMFMC serves as an advisory panel to the National Marine Fisheries Service (NMFS), which is the federal agency responsible for managing natural resources in federally controlled waters. GMFMC officials come up with regulatory proposals and forward them to NMFS, which makes the final decision.

The RDAP is one of several GMFMC sub-councils that advise on policy. There are similar panels for pelagic species and blue crabs. (The Acronym Club meets each Wednesday at the local VFW hall.) These panels consist of biologists, commercial fishermen, fishing industry retailers, and, usually, at least one token sport angler. Representatives of the sport fishing community mostly regard the panels as dominated by commercial interests.

After looking at this "limited commercial season," the cynicism is easily understood. If put into place, it would involve a set overall poundage or trip quota of redfish to be harvested for commercial purposed from Gulf waters. As much as 200,000 pounds of redfish might be taken annually over five years.

According to Peter Hood of the GMFMC, they based the proposal on a lack of knowledge of redfish stocks in the Gulf of Mexi-

Stocking redfish has been one of the Texas Parks & Wildlife Department's most successful programs.

co: "Redfish stocks in open waters of the Gulf are sort of like black holes; we don't know much about them. One of the roles of our council and the RDAP is to determine where stocks are healthy or unhealthy. Government officials in various states banned redfish as a commercial species 20 years ago because they were in trouble. In the inland state waters, redfish seem to be recovered, but we just do not know what their status is in the Gulf. This proposal, which is sort of in a state of limbo, was made to help further research of the species."

NMFS and all the other fisheries panels are strapped for cash and do not have the money to do a full-blown redfish population study. The idea behind a "limited commercial season" would be to put scientists aboard the boats to tag and release some of the reds and study other aspects of the populations. "The commercial fleet would essentially be providing the boats and some of the manpower," according to a GMFMC document. The fisheries people would only have to pay for on-board biologist and limited supplies. It would be a cost-saving measure, or at least that is the idea. With snapper and other species like grouper in the spotlight, there's not much funding for redfish."

The document further recommends:

• Scientists need to know the age composition of adult reds in offshore waters.

• The absolute abundance of adult red drum in the Gulf of Mexico needs to be accurately measured.

• Random sampling of the commercial and recreational catches for age composition data is needed.

• Standardized stock assessment methodology needs to be developed that can accept area- (state-) specific data and work with these within the context of a Gulf-wide stock assessment.

• State-specific contributions of red drum to the offshore

adult stock need to be determined

• Angler-release and shrimp-trawl by-catch mortality and the ages or lengths of caught and released fish need to be determined.

• The length composition of the commercial catch (if put in place) needs to be measured.

Officials would use the research to study the schools of huge, sexually mature redfish roaming Gulf waters. This would make up the base of any possible future commercial catch, but there is another factor involved. On the Texas and Louisiana Gulf Coasts, increasing populations of juvenile (5- to 10-pound class) redfish are showing up on angler's lines. Charter boat captains seeking to catch red snapper and other offshore species are abandoning some oil platforms and wrecks due to the dominating presence of these redfish. The anglers are leaving these areas because redfish are illegal to harvest, no matter what size, in federally controlled waters. What is strange about this is that scientists believed redfish to live in the bays until they are past the 5- to 10-pound size, and then enter the Gulf to live with other sexually mature specimens of their species. Large populations of Texas slot-sized reds in the open Gulf were unheard of until a few years ago.

Scientists are still scratching their heads as to what has caused this phenomenon. One theory is that oil platforms and other man-made structures have given redfish more habitat in the formerly barren waters of the Gulf. Bay-dwelling reds hang around oyster reefs and similar structure. Another theory is that redfish of this size are naturally occurring in the Gulf, but years of commercial harvest messed up the delicate population balance. Now, after two decades of commercial prohibition, some believe nature is restoring the natural order.

How does this possibly play into the RDAP's proposal? It could

Texas Parks & Wildlife Department coastal fisheries biologists measures a redfish at a dockside survey.

be a signal that redfish stocks are indeed "recovered" and attest to the effectiveness of the diligent fight sport anglers waged to protect redfish back in the 1970's. Redfish stocks may indeed be healthy now, but what the future holds is anyone's guess. Remember, the idea behind the study is to determine whether redfish stocks are large enough to justify a commercial harvest. That's right—they want to allow redfish to be commercially harvested to see if opening the species to the market once again might be feasible.

The scary thing with any of these bureaucracies is they are the only ones holding the books. In other words, what they say goes. While independent scientists say red snapper populations are more than healthy, they (the feds) continue to shut down that fishery for six months at a time. They also continue to allow commercial fishermen to have 51 percent of the quota, although the economic impact of lost recreational snapper fishing is far greater than the commercial market value. The same thing goes with many other marine species. Yes, redfish are a mystery, but allowing a commercial harvest to see if a commercial harvest is justified is simply intolerable.

Redfish stocks may indeed be able to sustain a commercial harvest, and to be perfectly fair, those fish do not belong to sport fishermen or anyone else for that matter—they are supposed to be a public resource. On the other hand, sport anglers are the ones who paid for redfish restoration through saltwater stamp sales, and funded massive stocking programs that increased overall numbers of the fish in Texas and elsewhere along the Gulf Coast. Sport fishermen have lived with restrictive redfish limits to help bolster this magnificent fish. The last time the commercial fishermen had a go with redfish, they nearly fished them into oblivion. That is not an opinion, but a documented fact.

There is a chance this proposal will never see the light of day, especially since it was shot down in 2001. Numerous other issues are taking up the time and resources of NMFS, and support for redfish conservation is still high among conservation groups and state fish and game agencies. At the same time, some of the people involved with those organizations are asleep at the wheel and let the Feds screw up red snapper fishing without much fight. Hopefully, they will not do the same with any new threat to the health of the redfish population.

Only time will tell whether we will see another round of the redfish wars that dominated the coastal fishing scene of the 1970's. If the battles do start, hopefully the redfish will come out the winner once again.

Chapter Eleven

Miscellaneous Tips, Tactics, and Trivia:

FILLETING REDFISH

Redfish have big, tough scales and are tough to clean for some anglers. I always use an electric knife and following technique.

Rinse the fish and put it on a fish skinning board that has a clip to hold the tail in place.

With an electric knife, cut the tail near the end down to the vertebrae and stop. Then cut down the length of the vertebrae all the way up to the gills. Make sure and leave behind a little thin layer of meat so you do not get bone with the fillet.

Next, cut the fillet from the tip of the gills area downward. Remove the fish from the clip and clip on the fillet. Cut down the length of the fillet, hugging the inside skin of the scale side with the blade.

Repeat the process with fish on the other side.

You might lose a little meat doing it this way, but it is much faster than any other method I have tried.

PROPER FILLET KNIFE USAGE

Texas Fish and Game magazine reader Don Collins
sent in this tip.

> *When filleting or cleaning different fish,*
> *you'll probably have to cut through some fairly*
> *heavy bone at some stage. To do this safely and*
> *effectively, never use your good filleting knife on*
> *bone. They have fairly pliable steel blades and can*
> *flex, causing them to slip off the bone and into the*
> *person doing the job. It will also blunt the edge,*
> *requiring more frequent sharpening, plus it will*
> *needlessly wreck your good blade over time. When*
> *cutting through bone, use a heavy-duty blade with*
> *a good sharp edge, and never cut towards yourself.*

The electric knife is an indispensable tool for any angler serious about eating fish.

LINE TWIST PROBLEMS

Line twist is almost unavoidable because it is caused by so many factors. Lures that twist, such as plastic worms with hooks off-center, spoons, and spinners, are common causes. You can also twist a line with a spinning or spin-casting reel when you continue to turn the handle while a fish is taking out line. Every turn of the rotor puts a full twist in the line.

No matter what causes the twist, it is easy to remove, according to the experts at Stren. They suggest you remove all terminal tackle from the line and troll the bare line behind your boat for a few minutes. The current running over the line quickly takes out the twist.

APPROACH ROUGH WATER WITH CAUTION

If you have been fishing for long at all, you have been caught in rough water, or will soon. One thing you will quickly learn is to take big waves one at a time. Each wave is just a little different, so you usually have to handle each one a little differently.

Sometimes, there may seem to be a rhythm to the waves, but you still have to study each one because a bigger wave may be coming up behind the smaller ones. If you are not alert, you can and will get your buns soaked in a hurry, or worse.

One way to navigate big waves is to slow your boat. Many anglers try to run rough water excessively fast because they want to get to safety as quickly as possible. If you take waves too fast, you may take water on board and possibly swamp.

Most experienced boaters power up the face of a wave, then

slow down as they go back down and accelerate up the next wave. You have to keep the nose of the boat up or you will cut right through a wave and take on water.

Catching redfish is great, but you have to be careful in the sometimes-dangerous world of the Gulf Coast.

Sometimes it is possible to run between the waves, taking each wave at a slight angle. This method can result in staying in rough water longer, but it may be the safest method to use.

Confidence in your experience is another major factor in learning to successfully navigate rough water. None of us enjoys being caught in conditions that could be potentially life threatening. Knowing that you are capable of navigating to safety really gives you better judgment.

Today's boat manufacturers have made handling rough water

Catching a redfish on a fly rod can put a smile on anyone's face.

Landing nets are necessary for serious redfishermen.

Surf rods are great for catching bull reds along the Texas beachfront.

These two cuties eye a bucketful of reds.

PHOTO BY GEORGE KNIGHTEN

Soft plastics grubs are great for redfish.

Chartreuse is one of the author's favorite redfish lure colors.

Most redfish tournaments demand the fish be no greater than 27 inches. Allowing 28-inchers makes things risky if a game warden is present and finds a little more length in the fish than the angler.

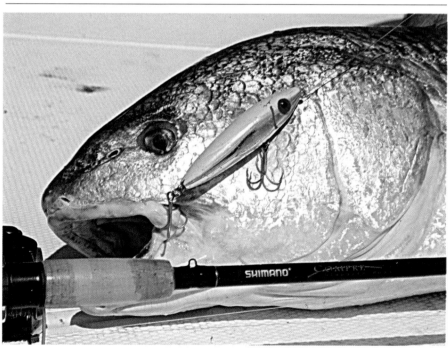

Mirrolures are hard to beat for any fish.

TEXAS FISH & GAME

Measuring a monster red in the surf at night can be tricky.

PHOTO BY GEORGE KNIGHTEN

TF&G co-owner Ardia Neves is all smiles after catching this massive redfish.

Wading stringer full of respects and specks are the stuff of dreams for many anglers.

Spinners are becoming popular for redfish on the Gulf Coast.

a lot easier by building longer and wider boats. The extra length and width add greatly to your safety.

Always think safety and common sense when fishing from a boat. Your life, or your partner's, could depend on your judgment.

MULTIPLE HOOK-UP TIPS

When saltwater fishing, multiple hook-ups occur frequently, and many times the fish are the same weight class. When two big ones hook up at the same time, let one fish run against a little drag on it and separate it from the other one. Letting the fish stay together is asking for tangled lines as well as one or both fish being lost. Fight them one at a time for the best results.

CARDS CAN HELP SUCCESSFULLY RELEASE REDFISH

Anglers kill thousands of bull redfish accidentally each year when they improperly release these big fish. Long battles stress these big fish and many times their air bladder inflates. This is a major problem when anglers catch them in deep water around oil platforms in the Gulf of Mexico. If you do not deflate the air bladder, the fish usually dies.

The matter has caught the attention of BOAT-US. Clean Water Trust, a nonprofit organization that provides helpful information for anglers and boaters. They are giving away free instructional cards detailing how to properly release these big, breeding-sized redfish. The group has said they will gladly send multiple cards to a person in hopes they will distribute them to their friends.

To order, call 1-800-BOAT-USA, or email jpereira@boatus.com.

REDFISH HOOKING TIPS

While fishing for bull redfish, most of what you catch will be released, so you must start using circle hooks. They always hook in the mouth and rarely gut hook. They are the best hooks for cut bait, live bait, and dead bait.

A good tip when baiting up with these hooks is to tie a knot tight on the bottom of the shank of the hook, using about 30-pound-test monofilament. This will keep the bait from sliding up the hook.

Also try mashing down the barb; you will be surprised that you just do not need it.

REDFISH FICTION

One book in a children's nature series by author Suzanne Tate is titled *Old Reddy Drum: A Tale of Redfish*. The publisher describes it: "Old Reddy Drum, a wise and powerful fish, gives life-saving advice to a young Peter Puppy Drum."

A HERO NAMED "REDFISH"

The image of big bull red rising to attack a topwater plug must have inspired U.S. Navy brass in WWII, for one of the most famous of the submarine fleet was christened *USS Redfish*.

The Portsmouth Navy Yard in Portsmouth, New Hampshire, laid her keel 9 September 1943, and launched her 27 January 1944 as part of the largest single-day launch of U.S. subs during WWII.

The site of schooling redfish is enough to make the author want to drop this book and go fishing now.

Redfish had an overall length of 311 feet, 6 inches; an extreme beam of 27 feet, 3 inches; a standard displacement of 1526 tons; a mean draft of 15 feet, 3 inches; and a submerged displacement of 2,391 tons. Her surface speed was 20.25 knots, submerged speed 8.25 knots. She had a design depth of 400 feet.

On one of its first Pacific patrols in the war with Japan, *Redfish* headed for Saipan teamed with *Sea Devil.* On the night of 8-9 December, the pair put Japanese aircraft carrier *Junyo* out of commission for the rest of the war. Dodging past escorts, *Redfish* made three separate attacks until the heavily damaged *Junyo* passed through the barrier of the Nagasaki minefields. Though not sunk, the carrier was damaged beyond repair.

The Japanese Imperial Navy sent another carrier to the Philippines, newly built *Unryu*, an 18,500-ton vessel rushed south by way of the East China Sea—more fodder for the mighty *Redfish* and its crew.

On the afternoon of 19 December, *Redfish* spotted a fast destroyer on the horizon, and an aircraft dropped a depth charge. A second destroyer soon appeared, then a Japanese carrier cleared the horizon and zigzagged toward the submarine. *Redfish* did not even have to alter course during her attack approach. Within eight minutes, four bow torpedoes struck and stopped *Unryu* dead in the water. The carrier opened up with all her starboard side guns while *Redfish* let go with four more torpedoes at an escort destroyer, which had passed just astern. The destroyer turned away from the torpedo wakes.

Shells and depth charges exploded at random while *Redfish* worked feverishly to reload. One steam torpedo aimed just aft of the carrier island brought thunderous secondary detonations from deep in *Unryu's* bowels. Clouds of smoke, flame, and debris enveloped the enemy carrier. *Redfish* dove to escape the fury of the destroyers—and "all hell broke loose."

Seven well-placed depth charges exploded alongside the starboard bow as *Redfish* passed 150 feet. Her steering gear jammed hard left. There was a hydraulic leak in the manifold, her bow planes jammed on 20 degrees up bubble, and loss of all hydraulic power. All sonar was off-line, and the pressure hull cracked in the forward torpedo room. There were numerous air leaks throughout the submarine, and a torpedo was making a hot run in the No. 8 tube.

The submarine came to rest in 232 feet of water, secured all running machinery, and waited out her pursuers. In a little more than two hours, *Redfish* was on the surface and running away from the destroyers at flank speed. The *Unryu lay* on the bottom along with her crated cargo of 30 experimental kamikaze rocket-bombs.

Redfish proceeded to Pearl Harbor, then to San Francisco, and later through the Panama Canal to Portsmouth Naval Shipyard. Her battle damage was repaired by 2 July, and she again sailed for Pacific combat. She arrived at Pearl Harbor on 22 July and was preparing for a third patrol when the "end of hostilities" came on 15 August 1945. Two days later, *Redfish* was presented with the Presidential Unit Citation for extraordinary heroism in action during her two war patrols. *Redfish* was also two Battle Stars for her actions.

After the war, the proud submarine served in training, intelligence, and special ops roles. Equipped with an experimental fathometer and a powerful underwater light, on 23 August 1952 *Redfish* became the first American submarine to operate an extended mission beneath the Arctic Ice, paving the way for a new era in submarine deployment. This adventure nearly ended in disaster as *Redfish* found herself trapped in a pack of drifting floes and heading toward "hostile waters." *Redfish* battled her way at conning tower depth back through the heavy seas of the Bering Straits and limped home to Pearl Harbor with damage to both screws and minus her torpedo tube doors.

The submarine's "special ops" included movie appearances. In 1954, *Redfish* starred in the Walt Disney production of Jules Verne's *20,000 Leagues Under The Sea*. Movie grips fitted her with a dummy rear fin for to mimic Capt. Nemo's *Nautilus* in one of the most dramatic sequences in the film.

In September 1957 *Redfish* starred as the *USS Nerka* in the MGM submarine classic, *Run Silent, Run Deep*. She finished her film career with several appearances in the popular black-and-white television series, "Silent Service."

After a long and distinguished career that included live saving and counter espionage missions, the aging *Redfish* was decommissioned in San Diego on 27 June 1968, her name struck from the Navy List 30 June 1968. Her stripped hull, like those of many sister vessels, was used for fleet target practice and sunk off the Pacific Coast. One of her former crewman described it as "a sad but fitting end for a brave fighting submarine."

Chapter Twelve

Tournaments:
Getting Green for Reds

Tournament fever is sweeping the Gulf Coast. Each year, thousands of anglers seek millions of dollars in prize money in tournaments from the Florida Keys to deep South Texas. The bulk of these tournaments center on speckled trout and offshore species, but redfish tournaments are growing in popularity.

In Texas, the most popular tournament involving redfish is the Coastal Conservation Association (CCA) State of Texas Angler's Rodeo or STAR tournament. The summer-long event features prizes for a variety of species, but awards the most sought-after prizes to those who catch redfish bearing tags affixed by CCA officials and release in Texas bays.

In the summer of 2003, Texas Ford Dealers gave each of the first five registered STAR participants who caught tagged redfish a brand new truck to call their own. The first five registered tagged reds weighed in received a 2003 Ford F-150 XLT 4-door Super Cab, and a 22-foot Blue Wave 220 Super Tunnel boat. Each boat-truck package included a 150 hp Mercury outboard and a Magnum galvanized trailer. The next five redfish weighed in received Blue Wave 220 Super Tunnel boat, motor, and trailer combos. Prizes like these draw thousands of participants to fish the STAR every year, and it helps generate good publicity and membership for CCA.

"The STAR is certainly our flagship event of the year, and is what gets our organization's name out in the public in a big way," said tourney director Bill Kinney. "Redfish are a very important part of the STAR, not only because of the prizes, but the fact that anyone can catch them. Anyone who fishes in a Texas bay has as good a chance to catch one of the tagged redfish as the next guy."

Many anglers in Texas sign up for the STAR for fear they will catch a tagged redfish and not be signed up for the tournament.

"It would be devastating to catch a tagged redfish and not be signed up," said Jay Watts of Laporte, Texas.

The Redfish Cup is a newcomer on the scene, has already helped put redfish in the national spotlight. The Redfish Cup events feature a top five cut after the first two days and a shootout-style finish to determine a winner. Days 1 and 2 see 110 teams competing for five spots in the final round. Berths are earned based on accumulated weight from Days 1 and 2. On day three, the final five teams start fresh with weights not carrying over from opening rounds. The heaviest Day 3 total team weight determines the winners. Tournament officials pair each of the teams with an ESPN camera crew.

Officials modeled the format after bass fishing tournaments, according to Jerry McKinnis, president of JM Associates, the media group that put the project together. "I believe we are not only getting ready to take redfishing to a new level, but we are taking competitive angling to a whole new stratosphere," he said.

Another group that looks to take redfishing to new levels is the Inshore Fishing Association with their Redfish Tour. The format is similar to the Redfish Cup, with venues ranging from eastern Florida to southern Louisiana.

Speckled trout rule the saltwater tournament circuit in Texas now but redfish are catching up.

Most tournaments involving redfish are not as grandiose as the big money events. I am not big on tournament fishing, but frequently fish the annual Orange County Association for Retarded Children (OCARC) tournament in my hometown of Orange, Texas. It usually draws between 200 and 250 participants, and redfish are one of the most sought-after species. The OCARC tournament for years allowed anglers to weigh in redfish requiring a trophy tag, but complaints from conservationists changed the format.

"There were a lot of people weighing in the big bull redfish, and since those are the prime breeders, we decided to stop allowing anglers to weigh them in the tournament," said longtime tournament director John Thomas.

Thomas instituted a 20-28 inch rule a few years ago, and in 2003 went to a 20- to 27-inch limit. "When that fish is 28 inches, it could go one way or the other legally, and we try to do the right thing by the law, so we put it at 27 inches to play it safe," he said.

Most tournaments allow only redfish within slot limits, and that is the challenge of these events. Unlike a speckled trout or bass tournament where a monstrous fish could get you in the big money, catching truly huge redfish is pointless in these events.

For years, I have covered the Saltwater Angler's League of Texas (SALT) tournament out of Port Arthur, Texas, and have learned anglers find it very difficult catch big redfish that fall within the slot.

"Everybody wants to get right on the edge and catch the ones right at the legal limit. And what is amazing is how much difference in weight there can be from one fish to another within an inch or less," said SALT tournament director Stan Armstrong.

I have seen reds at that event that were the same length, yet differed in weight by up to 2 pounds. "It all comes down to the girth," Armstrong said. "The angler that gets the fattest redfish at the tail end of the legal length limit wins."

That may seem easy, but in many areas on the Gulf Coast, catching a legal-sized redfish is difficult—and it is even more difficult when you want one right at 27 or 28 inches. Very often, anglers catch many 21- to 23-inchers and then the trend jumps up to around 30 inches. In fact, nowadays there are many redfish in Texas bays measuring more than 30 inches. When I was kid, that just was not a common occurrence.

PHOTO BY TOMMY LAMONTE

The Redfish Cup has given national attention to redfish competition.

"It's a miracle of modern conservation," said Texas Parks & Wildlife Department biologist Jerry Mambretti. "Redfish populations are very healthy and there are lots of big redfish in the bays. Things are better now than they have been in a long time when it comes to redfish."

That brings up a pointed question: What is the impact of tournaments on redfish populations?

"In Texas, we are able to stock millions of redfish. That, along with what Mother Nature produces, has kept redfish populations at high levels despite fishing pressure," Mambretti said.

Most redfish tournaments are catch-and-kill, and there is nothing wrong with that from where I stand. The population is holding steady, and as long as anglers utilize the meat or donate it to charity, they are committing no harm. Nonetheless, catch-and-release redfish tournaments might be the wave of the future.

Unlike speckled trout, which die easily if hooked or handled wrong, redfish are very strong, hardy fish that can survive in

Making sure a redfish is legal length in a tournament is part of a weigh master's job.

livewells for long periods. In a recent experiment, David Kinser of Oxygenation Systems of Texas and I kept three redfish alive for a full day of fishing in the heat of Texas summer in an oxygenated livewell. I then brought the fish home and put them in a holding tank, where they lived for a week before I put them on the grill.

"If oxygen is used from the time the fish is caught through the weigh-in, a catch-and-release redfish tournament could be very successful," Kinser said.

He should now. Kinser is involved in helping the Gulf Coast Troutmasters do live release speckled trout tournaments, which he admits is far more of a challenge than keeping redfish alive.

TPWD has created a tournament system that could be a blueprint for catch-and-release trout tournaments as well as aid trout conservation. Through an innovative program, called the Texas Gulf Coast Roundup, TPWD looks to saltwater anglers to target trout and other species during a series of fun and competitive angling events. Participating anglers receive awards for bringing in up to three live specimens from among 20 popular marine fishes, including redfish, spotted seatrout, and southern flounder.

"We want to make sure we take in the types and sizes of fish that are ideal for hatchery production, research, or educational display needs," said Mike Ray, TPWD director of coastal fisheries field operations. "Our staff spends a lot of time each year trying to go out and catch these animals. Frequently, the public has asked us how they can help and we wanted to find a way that we could utilize their angling skills, equipment, and time. We're hoping the Roundup will save a lot of staff time and help us obtain specific species we need. Once we learn how to better handle some of the offshore species, I hope we can expand this program to include some of the popular reef fishes."

HERE IS HOW THE ROUNDUP WORKS:

Participants may register in advance of each event using entry forms available at retail outlets with Budweiser Texas Gulf Coast Roundup displays. The events are open to anyone ages 21 and older with a valid Texas fishing license and saltwater stamp. Each participant receives a Texas Gulf Coast Roundup poster and may qualify for additional prizes.

Anglers show up at a predetermined location early in the morning to pick up aerated ice chests in which to keep their fish. After signing up, they set out to fish, and can begin turning in their catches from 10 a.m. to 2 p.m.

It is interesting that TPWD does not just seeking monstrous, genetically superior specimens. In fact, they target some smaller specimens on purpose. Prime candidates for donations include redfish between 20 and 27 inches in length. Good spawning fish does not necessarily mean extra large fish. "Sometimes, it is a matter of age and health. Saltwater fish are simply different animals from freshwater species," Ray said

TPWD held the first event at the Texas City Dike, while other events were held at places such as Pleasure Island on Sabine Lake. These are all top bank-fishing spots, and that is something Ray believes will be a big advantage for TPWD. "We wanted to include bank fisherman because they get left out of the picture in some ways. We also wanted to get them involved because there are some pier and jetty specialists out there that should be able to bring us some good specimens," Ray said.

Bank-fishing specialists have been some of the most helpful at these events. Members of the Elite Class Fishing School led by instructor Omar Garza were a big boost to the first-ever Sabine Lake event, which I helped to organize. They helped to bag some of the best catches.

Despite the increasing popularity of redfish tournaments, this is still mostly uncharted territory. Veteran bass tournament director Bob Sealy, who is now involved with the Redfish Cup, said it best: "Saltwater fishermen are a different breed from bass fishermen, and there are lots of different issues in the saltwater tournament world. The anglers are very dedicated and passionate, but they are generally a different crowd than tournament bass fishermen."

Whoever figures out those differences and plays to them will likely be making plenty of green out of reds in the future.

MAJOR REDFISH TOURNAMENTS CONTACTS

CCA STAR tournament

State of Texas Angler's Rodeo (STAR)

There is also a Louisiana STAR

Phone: 713-626-4222

www.ccatexas.org

The Redfish Cup

c/o Sealy Outdoors

Attention: Redfish Cup

P.O. Drawer 5431

Sam Rayburn, TX 75951

www.redfishcup.com

Redfish Tour

c/o The Inshore Fishing Association Inc.,

Jacksonville, FL 32257

904-733-6678

www.redfishtour.com

Chapter Thirteen

Wade-fishing

Sometimes, it simply pays to get in the water with redfish. This is an especially good method when a falling tide reveals redfish actively feeding in the shallows with their tails or dorsal fins sticking out of the water. This allows for the exciting possibility of sight-casting.

My good friend, Lee Leschper, wrote an excellent article for the April 2003 issue of *Texas Fish & Game* magazine called "Beginner's Guide to Wade-fishing." I thought it would be a great way to begin a chapter on this exciting way to fish. Here it is, with permission.

The last shrimp went the way of the quart of his predecessors—one jiggle of the popping cork, and a swarm of pinfish ripped it to shreds.

Aching back and scorching sun pointed me toward the shoreline, a sloshing, thigh-deep, half-mile away. A single "barely" redfish followed me on a long stringer. I was burnt, parched, and salty as a 30-day ham.

I was in heaven.

Wade-fishing is the best way to catch trophy-sized Texas speckled trout and redfish. It is a cheap, easy alternative to boats and gas bills. It is also salve for the nerves, food for the spirit, and refresher for the soul.

Sadly, millions of Texans still imagine that saltwater angling always involves huge boats, winch-like tackle, and the constant threat of seasickness.

That is just not so.

Our favorite bay sport fish, the speckled trout and redfish, are shallow water denizens. They live, feed, and breed on the clear sand and salt grass flats. These flats, back bays, bayous, and estuaries are the richest waters on the coast, home to every conceivable form of fish and crustacean life, including the shrimp, crabs, mullet, pinfish, and croakers that game fish love.

Many of these flats are less than knee deep and too shallow for all but the shallowest running tunnel hull boats. In this skinny water, any boat traffic will spook the wary fish. Even a drifting boat throws a big shadow and a big profile across the flats.

A wade-fisherman, on the other hand, is silent and almost invisible. He can slip undetected to within feet of big trout. That is why many of the best guides on the coast—driving the best shallow-water boats money can buy—still wade-fish. All the state record speckled trout fell to waders.

This is fishing stripped down to its essence—man vs. fish, in the fish's world. Tackle is likewise pared down to the basics:

• One trusted graphite rod—a 7-foot popping rod and casting reel or similar spinning tackle. Load the casting reel with 12-pound-test Berkley Big Game, the spinning reel with 10-pound-test Stren.

• Spare lures, including gold spoons, D.O.A. shrimp or mullet imitations, Cocahoe Minnows or Salty Assassins, and a few broken-back or Top Dog topwaters.

• Twenty-pound-test leader material.

• Popping corks or rattling floats.

• Floating bait bucket and No. 6 treble hooks for live shrimp and 2/0 Kahle hooks for live croaker or mullet.

• Small pocket tackle box.

• Needlenose pliers.

• Saltwater stringer with a healthy float at one end.

• Landing net (optional).

Travel light, but prepared. It's a long walk back if you lose the only bait that works. Your favorite bass rod will probably work just fine. Just remember that longer casts are important here, so lighter line and a longer rod yield more distance. Casting tackle is my favorite, but if you can get more distance from a spinning rig, use it. Most of the guides on the lower coast use spinning tackle.

Add a 2- to 3-foot shock leader of 20-pound mono at the end of the line to combat sharp teeth and abrasive shell. The reel should hold plenty of line and have a butter-smooth drag. This is no place to scrimp on quality. Saltwater is as corrosive as acid and will destroy cheap reels in no time. At the end of each day, wash your gear in freshwater and spray it with a lubricant like Corrosion X.

Remember that the wind usually blows on the coast. Wade downwind so you can always cast with the wind at your back. It will add 30 feet to your casts and eliminate backlashes.

A gold 1/4- or 1/2-ounce weedless spoon has to be the No. 1 lure on the flats. Add half of a strawberry tout for more buoyancy in shallow water. A spoon has lots of lift, and fished with high rod tip can slip along nicely in 6 inches of water. Lift the bait slightly with the rod tip, reel a foot or so, pause, and lift again.

Just as effective are the soft plastic shrimp and fish imitations. The Cocahoe Queen and Salty Assassin baits both imitate finger mullet and are superb wading baits. Rig them on the lightest jig-head you can cast, and retrieve them with that same start and stop retrieve. You can seldom go wrong with red-and-white, avocado metal-flake, chartreuse, and pumpkin pepper patterns. The D.O.A. shrimp and mullet imitations are equally deadly; inventor

Mark Nichols blended natural shape and action into deadly baits.

There is no dishonor in using live bait. Fish live shrimp 18 to 30 inches under a popping cork, just deep enough to reach the bottom. Hook the shrimp on a No. 6 treble hook just under the horn at the end of its nose and gently lob it out. Jerking the cork through the water like a topwater bass lure simulates the sound of fish feeding, attracting competitive trout. The cadence for popping the cork is a very personal, almost mystical matter. Some pop to the rhythm of songs such as "Happy Birthday" and "Mary had a Little Lamb." You want to pop just enough to attract attention without scaring away everything on the flat.

Live shrimp can be hard to find, especially late in the summer or on a busy weekend, and cost $8 to $10 a quart. They are hard to keep alive, but they work.

Live croaker and finger mullet are great baits for big trout and reds. These tough baits live longer and are not bothered much by trash fish. Hook croaker and mullet through the back just under the dorsal fin on a 2-0 Kahle hook. Then lob them unweighted into one of the creamy white potholes of bare sand you see out on the grass flats. Any red or trout in the area will nail it. Because of the size of these baits, you have to give the game fish time to get the bait into its mouth.

The key to whipping a fish on the flats is letting it run freely against light drag until it tires. Preset the drag just heavy enough to set the hook, and no more. Keep the rod tip high and let the drag and bend of the rod do the work. Wear the fish down before trying to net or grab it—a "green" red can wrap you in a cocoon of your own line. If you are keeping fish, string it before you unhook it.

When landing fish, grab them around the head at the base of the gills. Most saltwater game fish have sharp teeth so you cannot lip-land them.

Summer wading in Texas does not require fancy waders; old jeans and long-sleeved shirt or a light cotton one-piece jumpsuit work fine. Shorts are comfortable but do not provide protection from jellyfish. Old sneakers are the traditional footwear, but neoprene wading shoes are infinitely more comfortable and durable. The stingray-proof booties are even better.

Wear a long-sleeve shirt and cover all exposed skin with a good sunscreen. A long-billed cap is mandatory. Good polarized sunglasses are essential, both to protect your eyes and to help you see fish in the clear water of the flats.

There are more than 300 miles of shallow bays along the Texas coast and almost all offer productive wade-fishing, if you know what to look for. Trout and reds always follow the baitfishes. Look for flats with clear water and baitfishes, especially schools of mullet. Look for "nervous" water rippling with finger mullet or mullet jumping out of the water. Use you eyes and nose to locate oily, watermelon-smelling slicks made by feeding trout.

Sand and grass bottom is better than mud. Oyster shell draws fish, but is brutal on the ankles. A broad shallow flat adjacent to deeper water, whether the Intracoastal Canal or deeper bay waters, is always a good bet. Flats near a pass (a channel connecting the bay to the Gulf of Mexico) or between a main bay and smaller secondary bay are always productive at some time during the day.

Early and late in the day, game fish move shallower. They follow tides any time of day. High tide, when water is moving into the flats and carrying bait with it, is the best time to fish shallower.

Low tides, when the water is moving out, are best for fishing deeper flats, or the passes themselves. As the summer heats up, fish move deep earlier in the day, so be on the flats at first light.

Boat traffic drives fish deeper, but undisturbed redfish may be in shin-deep water anytime of day. Keep moving and looking. If one flat is barren of bait and game fish, don't waste time there.

Even if the fish evade you, the waters will embrace you like a mother finding a lost child. The gentle waves and singing breeze, the skittering baitfish and scuttling crabs, the gulls laughing overhead and the taste and smell of salt will take root in your soul.

GEARING UP

As Lee pointed out, while wading for reds, it is important to wear the proper attire and that starts with good footwear. Proper wade-fishing footwear completely covers and protects your feet from shells and other harmful objects. I often use old sneakers, partly because I am cheap, and partly because they work just fine. Numerous companies make wade-fishing booties designed specifically for this purpose. I am partial to the "Water Tennies" made by the Five Ten company. They have a neoprene mesh top and a hard rubber bottom. This allows the foot to breathe a little but at the same time gives solid protection. I use these during the late spring and early summer and then switch to my old sneakers worn over neoprene waders in fall and winter.

During winter months, neoprene waders are must-have. Catching redfish is cool and everything, but hypothermia is not. Waders are also good for protecting against stingrays and other hazards, which we will get to later. Nowadays, I wade-fish with a life vest on and consider it a necessary tool in the wade-fishing game. Yes, most of the time you will be wading in shallow water, but many things can happen. The tide could pull you into deep water, or the wake of a ship thrown onto the flats from a ship channel could knock you back. Then again, it could pull you toward it.

Wading belts are a must-have item because they allow you to carry everything from pliers to lures while fishing. More importantly, they give you back support, which is very important in wade-fishing. A day wading can be hell on the lower back, so you need all the support you can get.

I own good wading belts from Numark and Wade-Aid and recommend both. The Wade-Aid also serves as a floating device, although not Coast Guard certified, and is good for an added safety measure.

I carry a little homemade strap on tackle box that holds a half-dozen hard lures, has a compartment for plastics and jigheads, and strap for my needle-nose pliers. There are lots of wading gear boxes on the market. Some are good and some are junk. My best recommendation is to use a small, light box and carry as few lures as you can get away with.

STINGRAYS

Stingrays are the single greatest threat to wade-fishermen. Although not a vicious animal by nature, it can inflict severe pain with its "barbed" stinger if a wader steps on it. The best way to avoid a stingray hit is to shuffle your feet while wading. Many anglers call this the "stingray shuffle," and while it may feel silly, it can save you a lot of trouble and an expensive hospital bill.

While wade-fishing the Chandeleur Islands in 1998, I waded out from an island back to our boat. Just as I was about to step into the boat, I noticed a massive ray right in front of my foot. Had I been stepping, I would have been on my way to the hospital. But because I was shuffling, the big, ugly thing scooted in the other direction.

As many anglers on the coast of Florida say: "Keep your feet on the bottom."

Something to keep in mind is that most stingrays are invisible to the naked eye. They are masters of camouflage and can be under your feet without you ever knowing. If you see a few rays around, there is a good chance there are dozens or maybe hundreds in the vicinity. To counter this potential threat, some companies now produce stingray shields and stingray proof boots. Some anglers feel they are too cumbersome to wear, but I have a feeling those who have been hit by rays would disagree.

Anglers wanting to keep fish will have to invest in either a floating stringer or a floating ring with a fish basket. I advise using the latter because sharks love to attack fish on stringers. Sometimes they will hit the baskets, too, but your chances of an encounter with "Jaws" will greatly decrease.

Perhaps even more important than what type of device you will use to keep the fish on is how long the rope is. I now go with a 35-foot rope to attach my float ring to the wading belt. An encounter with a big shark in the Chandeleur Islands got me to wanting my fish as far away from me as I can get them. In case you have not noticed, that area is very wild and untamed with lots of potential dangers. The fishing there is magnificent, so the ends justify the means.

And that is sort of the theme with wade-fishing, because it is not for everyone. If you have never seriously pursued wade-fishing, you might consider it strange to soak oneself in saltwater and deal with possible encounters with hazards like stingrays when boats offer more comfort and allow you to cover more ground more quickly. But that is exactly what dedicated waders do not like.

From my standpoint, I see stealth as a very important aspect of wading. Because walking in saltwater can be flat-out tough, wading forces the angler to fish slower and look at an area differently.

Being in a more intimate relationship with your surroundings creates a different perspective, and sometimes, that is what it takes to get anglers to see the little things that can lead to limits of reds.

Thanks and Acknowledgments

Writing a book is an arduous task and while I was ultimately responsible for creating it, there are many whose guidance, hard work and inspiration made it all possible.

First, I would like to thank my Lisa who is the perfect mate. She has always been understanding and supportive and never questions me when I go off on some fishing or hunting adventure. She knows when I am in the outdoors I am at peace.

My parents were and are a big source of inspiration for me. My Dad introduced me to fishing when I was really young and my mother always supported our fishing efforts. I love you both deeply.

My grandmother Ruby Pickard was a big part in my upbringing and helped instill values in me that have helped me to stay afloat in the tough business of outdoor writing.

I am fortunate to have a number of people I call true friends. I do not throw that word around lightly and when I call Chris Villadsen, Lewis Hogan, Patrick Trumble, Todd Sonnier, Shelly Johnston, Jym Evans, Justin Tullier, and Clint Starling friends, I mean it; I love all of you guys. Thanks for always being there for me and putting up with my extreme views on everything.

Frank Moore is my cousin, but he has been more like a brother over the years. We have caught many, many fish together and will hopefully catch many more in the future.

Capt. Skip James taught me more about the business side of outdoor writing than anyone has, and for that I am eternally grateful. Over the years, we have backed each other when no one else would and for that he will always be like a crazy older brother to me. You will always have a friend in me.

Ed Holder took me under his wing to mentor me in writing back in the mid 1990s and greatly improved my writing skills and taught me to question everything I read much to the disdain of various officials and agencies.

Don Zaidle as an editor is like the drill sergeant in full metal jacket. He cracks a mean whip, but is an excellent editor and has helped me improve my craft. Plus, I once saw him pick up a big, nasty rice rat in the field and dispense it with a knife. That alone makes him cool in my book.

Thanks to Roy Neves, Duane Hruzek and everyone at Texas Fish & Game for believing in me and giving me the opportunity to write this book.

Larry Bozka gave me a chance five years ago and I ran with it. We do not talk much these days but I am still grateful.

Thanks to Keith Warren for being a good guy and for taking me to some awesome destinations. Also, thanks for representing the support like you do.

I would like to thank Eric Adams of my favorite band *Manowar* for being a great guy, sharing a serious passion for bowhunting and for singing the most uplifting, inspirational music of all time. I would also like to thank his manager John Pettigrass for being a cool guy and Joey Demaio for inspiring me to be a better bassist and for writing "Master of the Wind".

Ted Nugent has been my friend since I was 19 years old and I would like to thank him for inspiring me to stand up for what's right and for showing that compromise means losing in the world of gun and hunting rights.

Thanks to Ronnie James Dio for making music that carried me through dark times and to Pantera for writing music that is great to work out too. Sometimes its hard to make yourself bench press 250 pounds, but when you have *Pantera*'s "A New Level" blasting it does not seem so bad.

Thanks to Sean Hannity for writing "Let Freedom Ring" and for defending conservative values and American liberty against the onslaught of liberalism.

Thanks goes out to my tae kwon do instructor, fourth degree black belt David Howells for pushing me to be a good martial artist and enhancing my discipline. Also thanks to the other instructors from the Orange and Beaumont Tae Kwon Do academies, Paul Ferris, Valerie Bailey, Ryan Cedars, Jason Pollock and to all of my sparring partners. It is amazing we fight every week and never get mad. That says a lot for the sport.

There are many people in the outdoors industry to thank for various support over the years. "Wild" Bill Skinner of Bass-N-Mexico is one of my favorite people and is crazier than me. That says something about both of us!

Thanks to Kimbra Pierce, Lee Leschper, Mark McDonald, Johnette Childs, Burt Rutherford, Darryl Laurent of Mr. Twister, Bruce Stanton of Pradco, Karen Anfinson, Gary King and Brian Thomas of Pure Fishing, Mark Davis of Shakespeare, TJ Stallings with Daiichi Tru-turn, Ken Chaumont of Bill Lewis Lures,

Trey Kistler of Kistler Rods, Sharon Andrews of Storm Lures, David Kinser of Oxygenation Systems of Texas, Ken Zwahr of Lakes of Danbury, Tony Gergely of Surelife Labs, Fred Epperson of Numark, Durwood Adams, Woody and Russell with Snapper Slapper Lures, Allen Ray and Besty Moers of the Surf Court Motel in Rockport, Capt. Daniel Pyle of Stateline Guide Service, Keith Warren and Gerry Olert of the Texas Angler, Rob Harrell of Travis Marine, Reid Ryan, George Calhoun and Matthew Gregory of Wade-Aid Enterprises, Mark Nichols of D.O.A. Lures, Ben Jarrett at Skeeter, Will Beaty and Troy Coleman of Central Flyway Outfitters, Rian Glasscock and Todd Bryson, Gary McElduff of Texas Guides, Jim Leavelle, Don Wood, Doug Pike, Gary Ralston, Nick Gilmore, Claud Colston, "Wild" Bill Skinner, Mike Wheatley, Roger Bacon, Todd Masson, Ann Taylor, Ed Snyder, Jacob Elias, Bill Chapman, Sr. and Billy Jr., Thompson Temple, and Matthew Newman and Dennis Keller of Evolved Habitats.

Thanks goes out to my grandfather John Pickard for his tireless efforts with the Sabine River Basin Corporation to ensure clean an safe waterways for the public.

Thanks goes to Ryan Warhola for being as nuts for offshore fishing as I am.

Glynn Walker of Trophy Hunter's Archery deserves thanks for working with me on several projects and for representing our sport in a very positive way.

I would like to thank the men and women of the United States armed forces for defending freedom. I pray for you every day.

Last but definitely not least; I would like to thank God for breathing life into me and for giving me wisdom and strength. I am perpetually in awe of your creation.

Index